Hudson Bay

Atlantic Ocean

QUÉBEC

NEWFOUNDLAND

NEW BRUNSWICK

Saint John

Montreal

D

A

Ottawa

VER.

NEW HAMPSHIRE

MASS.

Boston

CONN.

RHODE ISLAND

WISCONSIN

MICHIGAN

NEW YORK

Grand Rapids

New York

NEW JERSEY

Milwaukee

PENNSYLVANIA

Chicago

Pittsburgh

DELAWARE

Moines

Toledo

OHIO

MARYLAND

A

Indianapolis

Cincinatti

Washington DC

WEST VIRGINIA

VIRGINIA

MISSOURI

Louisville

St. Louis

KENTUCKY

NORTH CAROLINA

TENNESSEE

Nashville

ARKANSAS

Memphis

SOUTH CAROLINA

Little Rock

ALABAMA

Atlanta

MISSISSIPI

Birmingham

GEORGIA

LOUISIANA

Jackson

Jacksonville

New Orleans

FLORIDA

Gulf of Mexico

Miami

D0601654

Zone 1 below −50°	Zone 3 −35° to −20°	Zone 5 −10° to −5°	Zone 7 5° to 10°	Zone 9 20° to 30°
Zone 2 −50° to −35°	Zone 4 −20° to −10°	Zone 6 −5° to 5°	Zone 8 10° to 20°	Zone 10 30° to 40°

DJDodds
January 1992

CLIMBING ROSES

Dedication
To my dear wife
for her support, understanding and toleration
of my time-consuming hobby.

WINTER PROTECTION

Hybrid tea roses grown in Zones 8, 9 and 10 have no special winter requirements. However, those grown in Zones 6 and 7 may require protection, and those grown in Zone 5 and colder should definitely be covered. If you live in an area in which the temperature falls below 20°F for any length of time and there is no covering of snow, protect your roses after winter pruning by building up a layer of soil (brought from elsewhere in your garden) to cover them to a depth of approximately 12 inches. Do not remove the cover until the ground is completely thawed.

SERIES EDITOR · VINCENT PAGE

CLIMBING ROSES

CHRISTOPHER WARNER

The Globe Pequot Press

Chester, Connecticut 06412

First American edition published in 1988 by The
Globe Pequot Press, Chester, Connecticut 06412.

Library of Congress Cataloging-in-Publication Data

Warner, Christopher (Christopher H.)
Climbing Roses

(Classic garden plants)
Bibliography: p.
Includes index.
1. Climbing Roses.   I. Title.   II. Series.
SB411.65.C55W37   1988   635.9′33372   87-32547
ISBN 0-87106-731-5

Produced by the Justin Knowles Publishing Group,
9 Colleton Crescent, Exeter, Devon, England

Design: Gilvrie Misstear
Photographs: R. C. Balfour and Vincent Page
Illustrations: Vana Haggerty
Zone map courtesy of Swallow Publishing Ltd

Manufactured in the United Kingdom

CONTENTS

Acknowledgements

I should like to thank all the people who have helped with this book, especially: Dick Balfour, for his wonderful slides and for his efforts to obtain pictures of the some of the lesser known climbers; Frank Buckley, for research into growing climbers in harsh winter conditions; Percy Hunt of Arizona, U.S.A., for detailed information on the world's largest rose; Ian Marshall, for a photographic record of the climbers at Mottisfont; Bernhard Mehring, for details of methods of growing climbers in northern Europe; Vincent Page, for photographs and much useful and constructive discussion; the rose firms of Delbard, Kordes & Tantau, for information and slides; the staff of Newton Abbot Library, for searching for old and new books; Graham Thomas, for locations of many of the older climbing roses; and Terry Underhill of TSW, for much helpful advice.

FOREWORD

What can one say about such a charming book as this? First, one is attracted by the numerous colorful illustrations, many of them by my good friend Dick Balfour. Then one is intrigued by the text by Chris Warner.

I met Chris Warner in July 1987 at the Summer Rose Show at St Albans, England. Of course, we talked of roses, and he took me out to the trials where two of his new seedlings were growing – miniature climbers, about six feet high. He sent me budwood of them, and I have young plants growing in my own trials.

As I read Chris' word descriptions of the many climbing roses, I could sense his very close and intimate relationship with, and appreciation of, each one. Page after page, one is made to feel as though the author is introducing members of his family. There is truly a bond between the man and his roses.

I especially like the format of the book as it progresses, one step at a time. Beginning with a brief history of several of the species roses, we are given a guided tour through the development of climbing roses. From some of the earliest crosses made to create new and better varieties, we are taken through the story of climbing roses right up to some of the favorites of today.

The section on cultivation covers all areas of the subject. Each topic is addressed in simple and direct terms and includes line drawings to illustrate planting, various methods of supporting climbers and also how to start new plants from cuttings and by budding on understocks. Hybridizing, the art of starting a new variety from seeds produced by hand pollination, is also dealt with in a simple and clear way in both words and drawings.

Then there is a section entitled One Hundred Climbing Roses, in which the author describes his favorites among the climbers. He begins with several of the species (wild) roses that make attractive garden subjects and carries the reader along the path, introducing other favorites from years past, before bringing us right up to some of the more recent introductions. I have lived with roses all my life, and so I enjoyed the descriptions of the various roses, many of them familiar to me from years past.

Reading this book has been an exciting experience for me in several ways. It has reminded me of occasions when I met some of these rose friends in the past. I have actually at different times grown in my own garden many of the roses Chris Warner describes. I remember the huge plant of yellow Banksiae, which my mother grew from a cutting. Then there were *Rosa bracteata* and its offspring 'Mermaid', which I grew on a fence. Many years ago I had *R. wichuraiana*, which I let spread out on the ground under several other climbers. My own cross of *R. wichuraiana* × 'Floradora' gave me a row of seedling ramblers, of which I saved only one plant, a single pinkish-apricot colored rose. This, when crossed with a miniature seedling, became the foundation for breeding many of the miniatures of today, including the ground cover/climber 'Red Cascade'.

I remember the lovely 'Emily Gray', and I still have Climbing 'Cécile Brunner'. 'Maréchal Niel' and 'Paul's Scarlet' grow in my garden today. And you either like it or hate it ... the old rambler 'Veilchenblau', which I grew many years ago. Then there are several lovely climbers from more recent breeding such as 'Dortmund', 'Golden Showers', 'Handel', 'Rosarium Uetersen', 'Royal Sunset' and others.

Although this book is written from a British point of view and omits several good climbers that are widely available on the American market, it is, nevertheless, well worth adding to your rose library.

Ralph S. Moore, D.H.M.

INTRODUCTION

The climbing rose is sadly overlooked in most gardens. Drive down any street or enter any housing estate and see how many houses have climbing roses in their front gardens or against a wall. Perhaps one in fifty. But why should this be so? I believe that it stems from the mistaken notion that climbing roses are hard work and difficult to cultivate. This misunderstanding must have originated at least in part from the climbing roses that were produced at the beginning of this century. These did indeed need a considerable amount of care and attention. After flowering, most of the old wood had to be removed down to the base and the new growth tied in in its place. This meant untying, cutting out, removing with care and then tying in again. As many of these roses grew 12–15ft (3.7–4.6m) each year, this represented quite a formidable task. But most of the climbers that have been bred since 1930 are much simpler to look after. By and large, they are of upright but restrained growth, and the only pruning needed is to remove the dead wood and to cut to the desired shape.

If you choose your varieties carefully, spraying to keep away diseases will need be done only once a month, and you will need a few ties to hold the stems in position. Now what's difficult about that? Your rewards will be months of colour, fragrance and delight, and it won't be long before your neighbours are looking with envy at your garden.

Nearly every garden has a lawn. I expect you have one. Have you thought about how much work is involved and how many hours you spend looking after it? Cutting once or twice a week during the growing season, trimming edges perhaps twice a month, raking, spiking, spraying, watering and feeding. Is that enough to be going on with? You may have to go and buy fuel for your mower. Then the blades will need sharpening and the cutting height adjusting. You could grow fifty climbing roses, and they would still be less work than your lawn.

Consider next the infinite possibilities of the climbing rose. Most houses on new estates do not have very large gardens, and many do not have much more than a pocket handkerchief at the front. But nearly all of them have a wall space between the front door and the front windows. Here is the best place to have your first climbing rose. Choose one of the varieties with restrained, upright growth, some 7–8ft (2.5m), and for several months of the year every time you enter your house you will have pleasure and respite from the pressures of living. In the back garden there may be an uninteresting fence screening you from your neighbour. Here you should select a more vigorous lateral grower, which might in time adorn your fence from end to end. If you have a long fence, consider planting two or three varieties. Perhaps there is an old, no longer attractive tree at the bottom of your garden. Why not plant one of the more vigorous varieties that will climb up into the branches and produce cascades of sweet-scented blossom?

Almost the entire colour spectrum is represented among climbing roses, the only major colour not found being blue, although there are purple and mauve varieties, and from a distance "Veilchenblau" looks almost blue. There are scarlet, dark crimson, golden-yellow, lemon-yellow, cream and white, near grey roses, and now even a tan rose. You will find a colour to blend and harmonize with every type of background.

You will also find a climbing rose with a habit that will suit any type of situation. Some varieties grow straight up, with hardly any lateral growth; some grow much more sideways than upwards; some grow many feet in a year while others make only 2–3ft (0.9m) a year. They can be pulled and twisted, yanked sideways and tied down, wrapped round and round a support, hacked and pruned, knocked by passers-by and still they will grow. You can select a variety that will grow to 6ft (1.8m) or you can have one that will reach nearly 60ft (18.3m).

This book has been written for the interested gardener and not for the botanist. The language has been kept as straightforward and simple as possible and, where practicable, botanical terms have been avoided. However, a glossary of the most often used technical terms is included.

I hope that if you haven't yet tried to grow a climbing rose in your garden, you may be persuaded to change your mind by the pages that follow. And remember, even if we can't all own a cottage in the country, most of us can have a rose around the door.

Christopher Warner, Spring 1988

THE HISTORY
OF CLIMBING ROSES

Climbing roses were almost unknown to the western world until as late as the 19th century. Of course, *Rosa moschata,* the supposed musk rose of Shakespeare's day, would have been known to keen gardeners, but this is not a strong grower and, except for its scent, has little to recommend it. The United Kingdom has only one native climber – *R. arvensis,* a lax, sprawling rambler, which can form a large mound, trail along the ground or wend its way into the branches of a nearby tree. *R. arvensis* is not a striking plant, as its flowers are rather pale and are often produced singly, occasionally in small bunches. However, as it is usually in flower by Midsummer's Day, it is likely that it was this rose that Shakespeare referred to rather than the more fragrant but less well known *R. moschata.* Moreover, *R. moschata* does not flower until August in England, so unless Shakespeare was employing poetic licence, we must presume that *R. arvensis* was his musk rose.

There is one other European climbing rose, *R. sempervirens,* but this is not winter hardy and is unlikely to have thrived in many English gardens, although there is a report that it was introduced into England as long ago as 1629. *R. sempervirens* is a near evergreen rose, which originated in the lands bordering the Mediterranean. It has bright, shiny foliage and can achieve heights of 15–20ft (4.6–6.1m). It was a parent of "Félicité et Perpétué" (see pages 108–9).

The United States has one native climbing rose, *R. setigera,* known also as the Prairie rose. Tough and hardy, it is not a tall grower, reaching only 6–9ft (1.8–2.7m), and the dark pink flowers are not produced in any great quantity.

Towards the end of the 18th century increasing trade with China stimulated interest in all things oriental, including plants. Travellers brought back tales of rampantly growing roses in colours unseen in the west. However, the Chinese, suspicious of the intentions of the European explorers, refused to allow them to travel in their country, and the plant collectors were allowed few contacts, the principal one being through the Fa Tee nursery, which was near the city of Canton and close to the Chu Chiang river.

In 1792, in an attempt to expand trade, a British mission under the leadership of Lord Macartney went to Peking. Secretary to the mission was

George Staunton, a keen plantsman, and he was able to explore, with others from the mission, parts of the Shantung and Kian provinces. In 1792 they discovered *R. bracteata*, which became known as the Macartney rose (see page 99).

The first multiflora rose arrived in England in 1804. Sent by Thomas Evans, an employee of the East India Company, it was the form known as *R. multiflora carnea*, which has small, pale pink double flowers. This was a significant event, for this rose led to a race of new, free-flowering climbing roses. In 1817, *R. multiflora platyphylla*, supposedly a natural hybrid between *R. multiflora* and *R. rugosa* and known popularly as the Seven Sisters rose, arrived in England, where it is still found in old cottage gardens.

Seeds of the first single-flowered multiflora are believed to have been sent to France in 1862, where they reached Guillot, the nurseryman and hybridist. These seeds were the probable forerunners of the race of roses that we now call floribundas. *R. multiflora* passed on its ability to flower freely to its descendants, and, although they are only once flowering, "Blush Rambler", "Hiawatha", "Veilchenblau" and "Violette" are still worth growing. It seems a pity that no hybridist has attempted to produce a repeat-flowering multiflora rambler, but those qualities of fragrance and freedom of flower may tempt someone in the future. Before leaving *R. multiflora*, mention should also be made of "Crimson Rambler", which was discovered growing locally in a garden by Robert Smith, professor at the University of Tokyo. As it has also been found growing in China, it is probable that it originated in that country. "Crimson Rambler" was originally sent to Scotland, but it eventually reached the hands of a nurseryman in Buckinghamshire, England, who put it on the market in 1893. It proved to be a sensation, for nothing so colourful and free flowering had been seen before. "Crimson Rambler" remained popular for many years until its proneness to mildew caused it to fall from favour.

In 1803 the Royal Society sent William Kerr to China to look for new garden plants. He found a double white form of *R. banksiae* growing in a Canton garden, and this was named *R.b. banksiae* after Lady Banks, the wife of the President of England's Royal Horticultural Society. A few years later, the R.H.S. commissioned J. D. Parks to collect a second Banksiae rose from the Calcutta Botanic Garden. This had been brought to India from China, and one can imagine the excitement when this first flowered in England in 1824. This form, now known as *R. banksiae lutea*, was fully double and free flowering; it was also yellow, then a completely new colour in climbing roses in the west. It was not until later in the century that the single white and single yellow Banksiae roses arrived in Europe.

In the middle of the 19th century Robert Fortune, an English plant collector, made four journeys to China. Restrictions on travel were still severe, but Fortune, clearly a resourceful fellow, dressed himself like the Chinese, shaved his head and donned a pigtail. He was able to travel freely and discovered three new climbing roses, the most important of which was "Fortune's Double Yellow", which he found in the garden of a wealthy mandarin and sent to England's Royal Horticultural Society in 1845. This is a tender rose and only once flowering, but its amber colour with a coppery hue was new to climbing roses.

The last climber to be discovered in the 19th century was *R. gigantea*, which was found by Sir Henry Collet in the Shan Hills of northern Burma. It was subsequently also found in south-west China. Collet sent it to England where it was first grown in 1889. It did not, however, flower at England's Kew Gardens and in 1904 a plant at Albury Park, Surrey was the first to produce flowers in England.

The greatest plant explorer as far as roses are concerned was undoubtedly Ernest H. Wilson. Early in the 20th century he sent back to England a whole host of new rose species, some of which have proved both important and beautiful new climbers. Initially working on behalf of Kew Gardens, he was later employed by the Arnold Arboretum. His most important climbing rose collections were *R. sinowilsonii* in 1904, *R. helenae*, *R. multiflora var. cathayensis* and *R. rubus* in 1907, *R. filipes* in 1908 and *R. multibracteata* in 1910.

Plant breeders were thus supplied with a range of species from which to develop new climbing roses, but surprisingly few of them have been used. To date, there are no truly repeat-flowering hybrids developed from *Rosae banksiae, cooperi, filipes, gentiliana, helenae, laevigata, mulliganii, rubus* and *sinowilsonii*. In addition to the individual beauty and fragrance of these roses, they do offer the plant breeder an opportunity to infuse good health back into garden hybrids.

The first recorded cross, (*R. moschata* × "Parsons Pink China") with a climbing rose, was made in 1802 by John Champney of Charleston, South Carolina, and the rose became known as "Champney's Pink Cluster". A seedling from this rose, probably a self, produced the famous "Blush Noisette", which led to a whole new race of climbing roses. Louis Noisette initiated this work, but other French breeders quickly followed. One of the earliest hybrids to appear and still one of the best was "Desprez à Fleur Jaune", known also as "Jaune Desprez". It was introduced as long ago as 1830, and I recently saw a plant of this rose in the wall garden at Mottisfont Abbey, Hampshire, England. It was covered in bloom to the top of the 10ft (3m) wall and was spreading laterally over 20ft (6.1m). The repeat-flowering climbing sport of the bush rose "Aimée Vibert" appeared in 1841, and others of note were "Céline Forestier" in 1842, "Gloire de Dijon" in 1853 and "Alister Stella Gray" in 1894.

A number of climbing tea roses were raised during the 19th century. Some of these were climbers in their own right, others were climbing sports of bush roses, but all were distinguished by graceful nodding blooms in pastel shades of white, cream, fawn, yellow and orange. Few of them were winter hardy, and they needed to be grown under glass or in very sheltered, warm gardens. Noteworthy examples were "Fortune's Double Yellow" in 1845, "Souvenir d'un Ami" in 1846,

"Devoniensis" in 1858, "Maréchal Niel" in 1864, "Rêve d'Or" in 1869 and "William Allen Richardson" in 1878. Two outstanding climbing teas appeared early in the 20th century – "Lady Hillingdon" and "Mrs Herbert Stevens" – but the greater hardiness of the other new climbers meant that the endeavours of the rose breeders were concentrated elsewhere.

R. wichuraiana reached the United States late in the 19th century, and plants were distributed to several leading nurseries. One recipient was Michael Horvath of the Newport Nursery, Rhode Island. He was visited by Barbier from Orleans, France, and, no doubt impressed by what he saw, Barbier began hybridizing with *R. luciae,* a species closely linked with *R. wichuraiana.* Horvath produced several interesting winter-hardy climbers, but none of them gained international recognition. Barbier, on the other hand, came up with a winner straight away when he introduced "Albéric Barbier" in 1900. This rose can still be seen in countless gardens, making a prodigious display in the early weeks of summer.

From 1900 onwards a flood of new climbers was bred from *R. wichuraiana.* Most of the work was done in America, but Barbier continued to produce several wonderful new varieties: "Léontine Gervais" appeared in 1903, "François Juranville" in 1906, "Alexandre Girault" in 1909, and in 1921 perhaps his most famous rose of all, "Albertine". American nurserymen meanwhile had brought out "Dorothy Perkins" in 1901, "American Pillar" and "Minnehaha" in 1905 "Excelsa" in 1909, "Dr W. van Fleet" in 1910 and "Mary Wallace" in 1924.

"Dr W. van Fleet" proved to be an extremely important rose, for in 1930 it produced a perpetual-flowering sport. This rose, "New Dawn", marked the beginning of a new era of perpetual-flowering climbing roses. With the advent of "New Dawn", interest in *R. wichuraiana* as a breeding parent waned, but it is interesting to note that the Kordes nursery is working with it again to produce a new race of ground-cover roses. We might hope that this work will produce a new type of repeat-flowering climbing rose with lax, easily trained stems.

It was extraordinary that "Dr W. van Fleet", a once-flowering climbing rose, should produce a repeat-flowering climbing sport. Once-flowering ramblers occasionally produced dwarf perpetual sports, but never before or since has a repeat-flowering climber evolved in this way. "New Dawn", which is described on page 127, has had a tremendous influence on the climbing roses produced over the last fifty years, and although most rose breeders have now moved on to its offspring, some are still using it. Fine roses directly or closely linked with "New Dawn" include "Aloha", "Bantry Bay", "Casino", "Compassion", "Dublin Bay", "Parade", "Pink Perpétué" and "White Cockade". "New Dawn" has even played a substantial part in producing one of the healthiest large-flowered roses, formerly called hybrid teas, the shiny foliaged "Pink Favourite".

The most important breeder of climbing roses of this century and indeed, the most innovative breeder of all time was Wilhelm Kordes from Sparrieshoop, West

Germany, who might easily have been a nurseryman in the United Kingdom. He started a nursery in partnership with Max Krause in Surrey, England, in 1913, but on the outbreak of World War I he was interned as an undesirable alien for nearly five years. He passed the time by reading every rose book that he could lay his hands on and formulating much of his breeding strategy. On his return to Germany in 1920, breeding began in earnest, although his work with climbers did not seriously start until the arrival of *R. kordesii* (see pages 101–2). From 1954 hardy, well-foliaged climbers were sent to all corners of the rose-growing world. Kordes' first introduction, "Hamburger Phoenix", proved how greatly it was needed, for 40,000 plants were sold in its first year. "Leverkusen", "Wilhelm Hansman", "Dortmund" and "Köln am Rhein" quickly followed. "Karlsruhe" and "Parkdirektor Riggers" were introduced in 1957; "Heidelberg" and "Ritter von Barmstede" in 1959. "Morgengruss", my favourite of the Kordesii roses, was introduced in 1962, and the bright deep red "Sympathie" appeared in 1964. Wilhelm's son, Reimer, continued the work and introduced "Rosarium Uetersen" in 1977. Kordes' most recent trial ground award winner, "Kordista", which is not yet fully named, also has Kordesii in its blood, for "Goldstern" is one parent. "Goldstern", introduced by Tantau in 1966, is one of a series of climbers produced by the firm of Mathias Tantau from Uetersen, Holstein in West Germany. Tantau's first introduction was "Solo", a fragrant red "Crimson Glory" seedling and his most recent was "Lavinia", a large-flowered pink, introduced in 1980. The firm's work is continuing, and we may expect more introductions.

Several French nurserymen have introduced climbing roses during the last few decades, and the firms of Meilland, Delbard-Chabert, Croix, Robichon and Combe have all won international awards. Delbard-Chabert has had success with "Altissimo", a large single red, "Parure d'Or", with its yellow blends, and "Messire" and "Sensass Delbard", both with shades of red. The Meilland nursery has produced "Clair Matin", a soft pink rose, "Fugue", which is bright red, and "Iskra", which is known also as "Sparkling Scarlet".

Sam McGredy, who now lives in New Zealand, bred a series of successful climbers when he worked in Northern Ireland. His first success, introduced in 1963, was the soft yellow "Casino". This was followed in 1964 by the apricot orange "Schoolgirl", and in 1965 by his international smash hit "Handel", which is cream with a delightful pink edge to the petal. "Galway Bay" in 1966 was followed by "Bantry Bay" in 1967, both in shades of pink. The salmon-pink "Malaga" appeared in 1971, and one of his very best introductions, the bright red "Dublin Bay", in 1976.

Inevitably in this brief survey of the historical development of the climbing rose, several significant roses and one or two rose breeders have been omitted. Readers who would like more background should consult Roy Shepherd's *History of the Rose* and Graham Thomas' *Climbing Roses Old and New*.

Cultivation

Choosing your plants

Do not choose your plants from coloured illustrations on packets or from the illustrations in a catalogue. Ideally, spend some time reading about the available roses to narrow your choice, and then go to see them growing. If possible, go to one of the gardens that has a large selection of climbing roses (see page 136) and see for yourself the real colour of the rose you are thinking of buying (bearing in mind, of course, that this will vary according to the season) and its growing habit. If there is not a garden of climbing roses within reasonable travelling distance from your home, visit a rose nurseryman who should have one or two climbing roses in his demonstration garden. He should have a stock of one-year-old maiden plants, most of which will have flowers, and some of the larger nurseries have good displays of climbing roses.

Your choice of climbing rose will depend largely on the site available. If you have only about 8ft (2.4m) of vertical space, do not buy a strong upright grower. Does your site face north, south, east or west? Roses, like most garden plants, prefer sunshine to shade and need adequate supplies of moisture. One or two varieties, however, cope much better than others with an unfriendly environment, so if you have only a shady north wall, do not despair that you will be unable to grow a climbing rose. It is even possible to grow a climbing rose in a tub provided the soil is at least 15in (38cm) deep and you are prepared to water it regularly.

You must also consider the colour of the background: a dark red climbing rose such as "Guinée" would be completely lost against a dark brick or stone background, for example. Similarly, if you are planting a number of climbing roses side by side, avoid colour clashes. Red and vermilion do not generally associate well with pink, but yellow is an excellent blender and can be used to great advantage to break up colours that would normally clash, and even if you do not particularly like white roses, they can prove useful.

Preparing the soil

Few gardening books mention the importance of testing your soil before planting, but as at least 75 per cent of your success rate depends on the soil, it is essential to get it right. You can test your soil in a number of ways. First, watch it over a number of months. Does water drain away quickly or do pools of water stand for several hours after heavy rain? Is it sticky to walk on after rain? Does it shrivel and crack during dry periods? What colour is it? Ideally, your soil should look dark even when it is dry because a darker soil is not only richer in plant food but will warm up more quickly and start your plants into active growth earlier in the season so that the flowers are earlier. Soil can be improved over the years by adding farmyard manure, well-rotted compost, peat and even old soot.

Next, test your soil. Put a tablespoon of soil into a tall jam jar, almost fill the jar with water, replace the lid and shake it well. Wait ten minutes until it has settled, when your soil will have separated into its constituent parts. At the bottom will be small stones; above that a layer of sand; next the silt and clay; then the water, and finally, floating on the top, will be the decayed organic matter called humus. If there is a large proportion of sand, your soil will drain rapidly and quickly lose its supply of plant foods. You should mix large quantities of farmyard manure with your soil when you plant. If you cannot get farmyard manure, use peat and well-rotted garden compost.

If you find that you have more than 30 per cent clay, this need not be bad news, because clay soils are usually rich in plant foods, but you will almost certainly have to work harder because clay is both denser and more water retentive than other types of soil. If you have over 50 per cent clay, you will have to improve the drainage. Roses hate to have wet "feet", which prevent their getting sufficient oxygen to their roots. If you cannot lay drains, incorporate quantities of sand into your planting area, mixing it evenly into the existing soil.

If you have a very chalky sub-soil with only a thin layer of top soil, peat, farmyard manure and compost are again necessary. Treat very stony soil in the same way, but dig the lower spits as little as possible, instead using the organic material as a mulch. When you have discovered what type of soil you have, you need to find out how much plant food it possesses. Buying one of the soil-testing kits available at nearly all garden stores is money well spent. Unless you have a large garden, a kit will last for several years and enable you to assess, with a reasonable degree of accuracy, the food requirements of your soil and therefore your roses.

Plants obtain nutrients from two principal sources: organic and inorganic foods. An organic food is one that has once had life – a leaf, twig, apple core, sheep's wool, for example. An inorganic food is largely man-made from a mineral that has been chemically treated. Both types have advantages and disadvantages. Inorganic fertilizers are easier to handle and act more quickly but do nothing for the structure of your soil. Organic material is usually heavier and takes longer to work, but over a number of years will dramatically improve your soil's structure. Farmyard manure has the great advantage of improving the physical structure of all soils. In addition to food, it supplies air, improves the colour, enhances the soil's moisture-retaining qualities and increases the number of beneficial bacteria and worms. If you cannot obtain farmyard manure, build yourself a compost heap. Apart from the obvious things like hedge clippings, lawn mowings and leaves, you can add virtually all household waste. Do you throw away your tea leaves, banana skins, orange peel and meat scraps? What a waste! Of course, you should cover any fresh food by mixing it in with a fork that you keep to hand. And don't forget to cut up any discarded woollen clothing into small pieces and add them to your compost heap.

There is one other test that you should carry out on the soil in which you intend to plant your roses. Garden soils are acid, alkaline or neutral, which is a state exactly between acid and alkaline, and this is measured on the pH scale. A reading of 4.5 would mean that your soil was very acid; 7.0 would be neutral and 8.5 would be very alkaline. Most rose nurserymen use a rootstock called *R. laxa (R. coriifolia froebelii)*, which is easy to propagate as it has a long, straight neck and has the additional advantage of producing few suckers. To prosper, *R. laxa* needs a soil pH between 6.0 and 7.5.

Test your soil with one of the proprietary soil-testing kits or with a pH soil probe. These are comparatively inexpensive, easy to use and the probe produces results within seconds. If you have a very acid soil, correct it by adding ground limestone to the planting area. If you live in an acid area, you may have to do this every other year. It is more difficult to adjust a very alkaline soil, which is usually found in areas of chalk, but adding sulphur or large quantities of peat and farmyard manure will eventually correct the balance.

Using the right equipment
Your decision to plant one or more climbing roses in your garden need not involve you in any additional expenditure on new tools and equipment. However, if you do not already possess one, you may want to consider buying a long-handled shovel, or Devon spade as it is sometimes known. It has a blade shaped something like the spade in a pack of cards and a very long handle, set at an angle to the blade. I dig out over a thousand roses every year and move two or three tons of manure, and have been using one of these spades for the last three years. Its use has halved my work-load and saved me much backache. Of course, it is useful not only for moving roses around but can be used for all digging jobs except deep holes.

The only other equipment that I regard as essential to rose growers are two different types of gloves. Never handle roses unless you are wearing thick protective gloves. Apart from the obvious discomfort that will result from the occasionally vicious thorns, it is not unknown for gardeners to be infected by tetanus after being scratched by a thorn. You should also have a pair of thick

Using a Devon spade will allow you to adopt a more upright stance as you dig.

rubber gloves, which you should use whenever you are mixing chemicals and using a sprayer. Nearly all garden chemicals are poisonous to some degree or other, and it is impossible not to pick up a trace of a chemical from the side of the bottle after it has been used and this, of course, is in a concentrated state.

Planting your rose

Once you have determined what sort of soil you have and taken the appropriate steps to improve it or alter the pH balance, you are ready to plant your selected rose. Dig the planting area to a depth of 15in (38cm) and, if you are planting only one rose, to a width of 3ft (0.9m). If you are planting more than one climber, do not put the plants less than 6ft (1.8m) apart, and, if space is not a problem, they will look better up to 10ft (3m) apart. This is particularly true of lateral growers, which need room to reveal their full beauty.

Try to get farmyard manure, ideally at least one year old, to put at the bottom of the hole. On top of that put a thin layer of bone meal, followed by a layer of the excavated soil. Lay the roots on top of this, wedging the rose upright with a stake. Alternatively, place a broom handle across the hole and lightly tie the rose to it. The place where the branches arise from the neck of the rose should be in line with the general soil level. If you are planting against a wall, leave 15in (38cm) between the wall and the rose because the wall will not only prevent rainfall from reaching the base of the rose but will absorb moisture from the soil.

Cover the roots with a planting mixture of 50 per cent garden soil, 30 per cent peat and 20 per cent well-rotted compost or farmyard manure. If you have a very heavy, clay soil, you will need 30 per cent garden soil and up to 20 per cent coarse

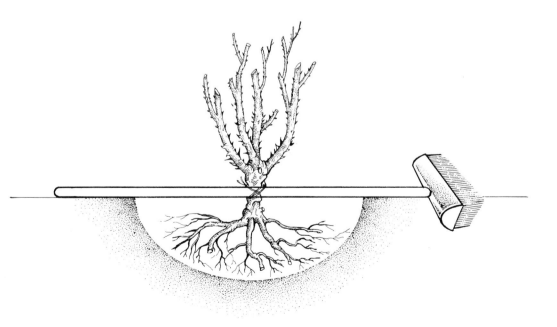

Place a broom handle across the hole and lightly tie the rose to it to stop it moving about as you fill in the hole.

builder's sand. If you have tested your soil correctly and found that it is deficient in one of the major chemicals, you may have to add additional plant food to the top 3in (8cm). An excellent all-round fertilizer is a mixture of blood, fish and bone in powder form.

While you add the planting mixture, shake the rose to ensure that there are no air pockets around the roots. Finally, tread the soil around the rose, but do not stamp – the roots need air.

Supporting climbing roses
Some people build intricate and decorative frameworks to support their roses, and very nice they look, but they represent many hours of work and they need maintenance. I am a firm believer in keeping the supports and the fastenings for climbing roses as simple as possible.

If you are planting against a single pole, make sure you buy a pressure-treated post with a vertical grain, which will last up to 25 years, as opposed to the five years or so of the one you treat yourself, and will quickly justify its expense. A post that is to stand 6ft (1.8m) above the soil will have to be buried to a depth of 2ft 6in (0.75m). To avoid damaging the pole, place a piece of wood over it to protect it from the hammering.

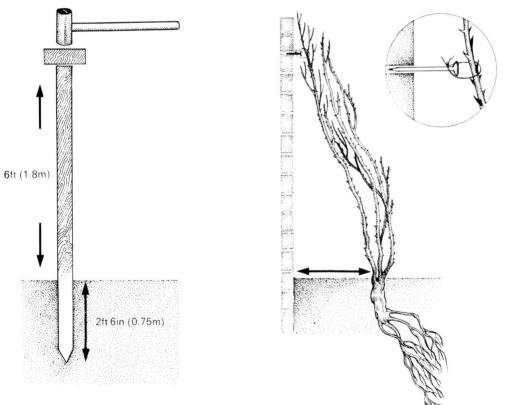

6ft (1.8m)

2ft 6in (0.75m)

Before you hammer in the post (far left), lay a piece of wood across the end of it to avoid damaging it.

Leave a space of about 15in (38cm) between the wall and the rose so that the roots are not deprived of water. Attach the branch to a wall nail with a loop of nylon cord.

If you are fastening a rose to a wall, most books recommend that you thread wire through eyes that have been attached to the wall with wall plugs. This method involves a fair amount of work, and, at least until the rose has clothed the area, is rather unsightly. A newly planted climbing rose can be held against a wall by epoxy resin plant stickers. While these are easy to use, they are effective for only two or three years, for sooner or later the combination of strong wind and the weight of the branch will tear them away. The simplest method is to use wall nails, which have larger heads than masonry nails. Once the nails have been hammered into place, tie nylon cord to each nail with a clove hitch and make a loop to hold the stem but at the same time give room for the branch to grow. The nylon cord will probably need to be replaced every three years. Make sure that the nail is sufficiently long to hold the branch at least 2in (5cm) away from the stone or brickwork, both to allow air to circulate and to stop the branch being damaged in a strong wind.

The problem you will meet if you want to grow roses against a solid wooden fence is that the supporting nails can be knocked into the posts but not into the panels. Plant stickers will, of course, support the rose for a few years, but probably the best solution is to drill small holes in the panels through which you can pass nylon cord.

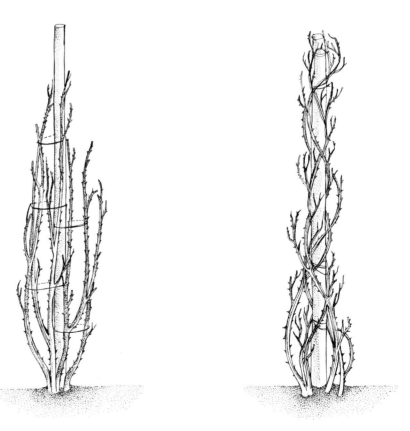

To train a stiff-stemmed variety such as ''Galway Bay'' (right), on which all growth is to one side of the support, tie in the shoots with nylon cord, but it is possible to train the shoots of a climber with pliant stems such as ''New Dawn'' (far right) around both sides of the support, again tying them in with nylon cord.

The frameworks that can be devised to support climbing roses are many and varied. I have seen roses scrambling into both deciduous and evergreen trees, but in a smaller garden you will probably grow a single rose against a post, or, if you have more than one rose, against a tripod arrangement of posts. You may be able to grow your roses against wooden or stone arches so that they ultimately form part of the arch, or you may prefer to train them to clothe either close-board or more open wooden fencing. Climbing roses are often grown against house and boundary walls, and if you are fortunate enough to have a steep bank supported by a wall, your rose will hang over and down the wall. In the absence of a formal structure, you might consider suspending ropes or chains from any height from 1ft (0.3m) to 10ft (3m) to support your roses. And do not forget that some varieties can even be grown as weeping standards.

Few of us have space for a pergola or catenary in our gardens, but those lucky enough to have such features may happily mix climbing roses with other plants. The blue shades of the clematis family offer the colour so greatly desired by some rose breeders, and wistaria and honeysuckle successfully blend and mingle.

The first years
Do not be disappointed if your new climbing rose fails to climb in its first season. More often than not it will appear to be making no growth at all, and this is because the root system is establishing itself, and until the roots have a hold, not a great deal of growth can take place. If you notice that what growth there is ends in blind shoots, it could be that some of the soil has subsided from the roots

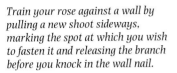

Train your rose against a wall by pulling a new shoot sideways, marking the spot at which you wish to fasten it and releasing the branch before you knock in the wall nail.

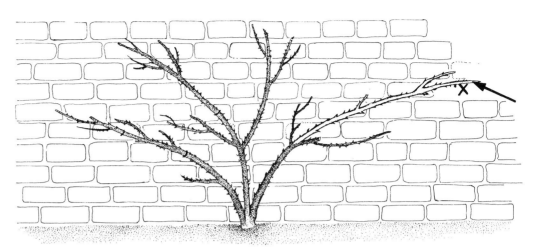

allowing an air pocket to develop. The simple remedy is to tread firmly around the base of the plant. However, if, at the end of two years, there is still no sign of climbing growth, you can reasonably presume that all is not well.

Climbers that grow vertically are more easily trained and tied to walls, pillars or pergolas than their counterparts that grow laterally. And although lateral growers will ultimately look more spectacular, their growth will need to be fastened and tied-in perhaps twice a year. They also need careful training. The growing shoot may well have to be carefully pulled sideways to get the shoot to the position that you would like. To achieve this, first slowly pull it sideways and feel the response until you reach the desired position, mark the fixing point and release the branch. Secure your fastener, attach the cord and then pull back the branch to be tied. It is better to fasten your shoots early rather than late in their growth, because even after as little as two or three months some climbers so harden their growth that they become difficult to train.

Feeding

It is probably by now apparent that I prefer organic to inorganic feeding. However, inorganic feeds offer a quick remedy if, for example, you discover a food deficiency or if you are growing in a small area, for tubs and spaces in a paved area can more simply and effectively be fed with an inorganic fertilizer. But the great advantage of organic material is that it does improve the physical condition of soil, and over the years you apply it, your soil will continue to improve.

Roses need at least one good feed each year; in some rapidly draining soils they may need two or more. You should feed when growth begins, although this will vary with the season and from region to region. However, as soon as you see the first sign of growth, put 3in (8cm) of well-rotted compost or farmyard manure around the base of each rose but not close to the stems. The only additional basal feed required is a light dressing of blood, fish and bone, which should be watered in during a dry spell.

Foliar feeds added to your sprays at approximately one-month intervals are of considerable benefit. Not only do they increase leaf size and therefore the plant's ability to photosynthesize, but they also increase the plant's resistance to fungal diseases. If you garden on a hungry, rapidly draining sandy soil, as well as a 4–5in (10–13cm) layer of compost or manure, give a further feed after midsummer of blood, fish and bone or a compound inorganic feed, watered in if necessary. Try to make this second application at least two months before the onset of the first heavy frost. If you have the time, extra foliar feeding, even once a week, will pay dividends.

Spraying

Spraying is a chore and one that I would gladly put off. However, if we wish to keep the leaves on some of our plants, spraying has to be done. Most manufacturers say you should spray at 10- to 14-day intervals, but this is rarely necessary. Adopt a spraying routine based on your own experience and requirements. You may, for example, find that while spraying at one-monthly intervals does not completely free your garden of insect pests, blackspot or mildew, it keeps the problems sufficiently under control for your own satisfaction.

Garden pests The pests that can attack your roses are almost too numerous to mention, and most of them will have a go at your roses at some stage or other. One of the best remedies is to encourage birds, particularly blue tits, into your garden by well-placed nest-boxes. Some birds will remove the caterpillars and aphids without your having to resort to spraying. However, if birds alone cannot solve the problem, you will have to use a spray. Remember, nearly all the insecticide sprays are poisonous; they should be handled and used with great care. Systemic sprays, those that are absorbed by the plant into the sap stream, are effective for up to two weeks. Contact sprays are usually effective for only a few days. Before you begin, read the instructions on the bottle to discover which type you have and how you should dilute it and prepare it for use.

Fungicides Friendly birds, insects and animals cannot help you keep blackspot, mildew and rust at bay, but good cultivation and watering during dry spells undoubtedly help. There is a wide range of fungicides on the market, some more effective than others. Among the best is one based on a combination of bupirimate and triforine. Again, read the small print on the bottle or packet before you mix the solution.

Sprayers and how to spray Sprayers are bulky, heavy and awkward to carry, so buy the smallest that will allow you to manage your garden. If you have only a few plants, a small hand-sprayer will be perfectly adequate. In the UK nearly all packets for spraying are based on quantities of 1 gallon (4.5 litre). This quantity inevitably means that the gardener with only a few roses and a small 1 pint (0.56 litre) sprayer is faced with the problem of storing his surplus mixture. If only manufacturers would produce smaller packets!

Wear protective rubber gloves whenever you handle chemicals. It is advisable to wear also an eye shield and clothing that can be washed after use. Only spray in calm weather, preferably in early evening. If any spray blows or drifts on to your face, wash it off immediately.

Climbers present special problems for spraying. Do not spray up into the rose, for sooner or later the spray will drift down on to you. It is more sensible to use a ladder or a pair of steps to get above your rose and spray downwards. If your sprayer is heavy, a shoulder strap is essential.

Pruning

Recently developed repeat-flowering climbing roses need very little pruning. Remove dead wood during the dormant season and remove old flower heads (dead-head) during the growing season, and you will find that the only other pruning necessary is to make the plant the shape you require. This may mean removing hardly any wood at all or considerable quantities – either way, the rose can take it. It is a task best carried out during the dormant season before any new spring growth begins. Make a slightly sloping cut above the bud that you wish to begin growing, and despite what it says in most books, it will not matter if you choose an inward-facing bud if that is the direction you wish the new growth to take.

Once-flowering ramblers flower for only three weeks. They are usually prone to mildew, and when flowering is over, most of the flowering wood should be removed right down to ground level and the new growth coming from the base tied in in its place. Once-flowering ramblers of this type do look magnificent for two or three weeks, but you may not feel that this is sufficient compensation for the extra work they represent.

Nicking

When climbers have been in place for a number of years, they can become bare and look unattractive at the base. There are two ways of overcoming this problem. The most drastic remedy is to remove a shoot almost to the ground, using a saw to cut first in one direction and then in the other so that the cuts meet. Do this to avoid tearing down the stem, which might result in stem canker.

The alternative is nicking, a technique for which we have to thank Dick

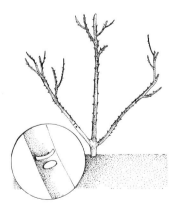

Nicking a branch above a dormant bud may encourage new growth.

Balfour. Choose a bud that is close to the soil and, in the dormant season, make a shallow nick right through the bark $\frac{1}{3}$in (1cm) *above* the bud. This nick should travel from one side of the stem to the other, covering about a third of the total diameter. It does not always work, but keep trying.

Replanting

If you should wish to replace a climbing rose that has been in position for a number of years with another, a soil transplant will be necessary. Although no one knows exactly why it should be so, if you fail to transplant the soil, your new rose will refuse to grow. When removing the soil, excavate down below 12in (30cm), preferably 15in (38cm), and over 2ft (0.6m) across. If you have a vegetable garden, take new soil from there. The old rose soil will grow good vegetables.

Growing in severe weather conditions

Normally in the United Kingdom the winters present no problem to the majority of climbing roses. During the winter of 1985–6, however, a freezing easterly wind blew for several weeks, and many climbers suffered severe damage, their stems killed right down to the ground. One group of climbers came through unscathed – those of Kordesii origin. In north Europe freezing winds are a regular occurrence, and nearly all climbing roses grown there are of the Kordesii type, which will survive temperatures as low as $-4°F$ ($-20°C$).

If other types are grown, they may either be treated as large shrubs, and the branches that are killed by the cold removed in the spring, or the branches may be clothed with twigs and small branches of fir, tied into position, which afford some protection from the chilling wind while allowing air to circulate. Straw and hay fastened over every branch has also been used successfully.

In northern parts of the United States and in Canada, some growers dig a trench some 2ft (0.6m) in front of the plant and then undercut so that most of the roots are enclosed in a ball of soil. The rose is then carefully lowered until the branches lie on the ground, when they are covered either with a mound of soil or with straw, bracken, fir, or wood shavings kept in place by a heavier material. Small mammals can be an additional hazard during the early spring if this system is adopted.

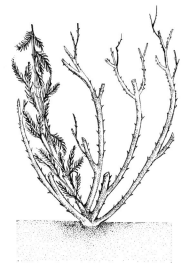

Covering branches with twigs and small branches of fir will help to protect your rose from severe winter conditions.

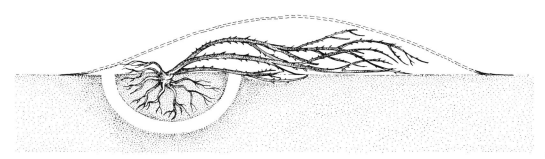

Dig a trench and undercut your rose; lay the rose at or below soil level before covering it with insulating material to protect it from extreme cold.

Root cuttings under polythene but remember to renew the air supply after about ten days.

Propagation

Nearly all climbing roses are propagated by budding (see pages 28 and 137), a very satisfying way of increasing your own roses, but they can also be successfully propagated by taking cuttings. Although this is usually done in England in September, if you root under polythene it can be done generally as soon as you have some mature wood. Cut wood that has hardened into 6–9in (15–23cm) strips. Leave one set of leaves at the top, dip each in hormone rooting powder and insert the cuttings in a trench with a little sand at the bottom if you have a clay soil. The trench should be 4–5in (10–13cm) deep and the cuttings 6in (15cm) apart. Not all will root, but you will be unlucky if one-third of your cuttings do not grow successfully. These cuttings will take a number of years to make a mature bush; budded plants will be bigger much sooner.

If you are rooting cuttings under polythene, use a largish pot filled with good quality, well-watered compost. Insert the cutting and tie a polythene bag around the pot. After about ten days give the cutting some air and then re-tie the polythene bag. After three weeks the cutting should have started to form roots. Give more air and remove the bag after about six weeks. These times are only a rough guide, for of course the ambient temperature will slow or increase the speed of rooting.

Hybridizing

Hybridizing is both easy and tremendous fun – Jack Harkness once described the time when seedlings are coming into flower, as "like having a birthday present every day". Nearly all hybridizing is done under glass, but climbers can be successfully hybridized out of doors in most areas against a warm wall provided the pollinating is completed before the end of June. The process of pollination is simple. Select your mother plant, and when the sepals enclosing the petals have

Successful hybridization is possible out of doors if it is completed before the end of June. First, select an opening flower growing against a warm wall and remove the petals and stamens. Between 24 and 48 hours later use a forefinger to transfer the pollen from the male parent. Two months later the seed pods will begin to ripen. Always label the seeds with details of the parent plants.

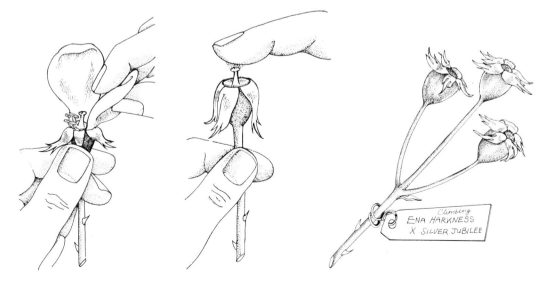

opened and turned downwards, remove all the petals and then all the stamens (the male part of the flower holding the pollen). If you are using a single rose as the mother plant, the stamens must be removed as the sepals separate because single flowers open very quickly. Next, choose your pollen parent. This can be another climber, a large or cluster-flowered rose, or even a miniature rose. Brush the pollen, using your finger or a paintbrush, onto the exposed stigma of the mother plant, 24 to 48 hours after removing the petals. Ideally, you are seeking to combine the characteristics of both roses, but an exact 50:50 combination rarely happens.

It is much better to have a clear objective when crossing one rose with another rather than just crossing to see what happens. Not all your crosses will take; if they get wet they certainly will not. Label your cross, mother parent first, so that your efforts are scientific.

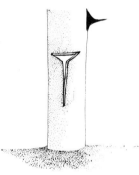

If you are a beginner, grow R. laxa (corifolia froebelii) as your budding stock as it has a straight neck and few thorns. Make a T-shaped cut in the neck of the stock $\frac{1}{2}$in (12mm) above soil level; gently prise it open with a knife.

Remove the bud from your chosen variety, cutting first below the bud and finishing above; the total length of the removed bud should be about $\frac{3}{4}$in (2cm).

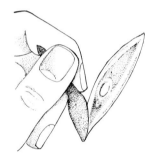

Remove the sliver of wood from behind the bud eye with your thumb and finger, making a downward movement until you are level with the bud and then twisting the wood sideways.

Holding the bud by the leaf stalk, slide it into the T-shaped cut.

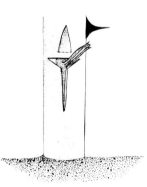
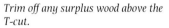

Trim off any surplus wood above the T-cut.

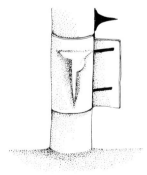

Fasten the bud securely in place with a rubber tie.

The seed pods should swell and ripen during the autumn months. If your seed pods are out of doors, they will take a little longer to mature, but they should be changing colour in early autumn and be ready to harvest a month or so later. If they are only just changing colour and hard frosts have already set in, they can be ripened further in a glass jar on a warm window ledge. Leave several inches of stem to prevent your seed pod drying out.

Sow your seed as soon as you can. It is not necessary, as some books suggest, to expose your seed to frost. Most rose seeds need a cool period, about 39°F (4°C), for three or four weeks, but frost only retards germination. From January onwards a little bottom heat, 50–54°F (10–12°C), is of great benefit. Rose seeds can be germinated in pots, trays, boxes, anything that you have available, and they prefer a light and airy compost. Sow no deeper than $\frac{1}{3}$in (1cm) and remember to keep your compost moist. If half the seeds germinate, you will have done very well. Do not be disappointed if your success rate is only 5 or 10 per cent: you will improve with experience.

Your rose seedlings should be grown on in 4in (10cm) of compost, so, if necessary, transplant them when they have two sets of leaves.

If you have used a repeat-flowering climber, nearly all of your seedlings will flower in the first year, and this is when your problems begin. You will want to keep all of them, but to be successful you must be ruthless and discard those that have dull colour, mildewing foliage, petals that refuse to fall and indifferent growth.

If you get addicted to rose breeding, join one of the specialist rose-breeding associations that now exist in the United Kingdom, the United States and New Zealand.

Nurserymen, Breeders and the Future

The world of bush roses is seeing tremendous change and development, and it seems certain that this activity will spread to climbing roses. It is interesting that nurserymen do not at present seem to have a clear idea of what they are looking for. Rather, they all seek varying types of plant, and this is perhaps a reflection of the enormous diversity of climbing roses.

Colin Dickson, of Dicksons of Northern Ireland, has reported that some interesting patio shrubs have appeared among seedlings without any deliberate intention to breed them. These shrubs have small flowers and foliage and reach about 4ft (1.2m), and Dickson sees no reason why these cannot lead to 6ft (1.8m) patio climbers, ideal for the small garden. The nursery has tried to produce larger climbers from "New Dawn" but without success, and it is also trying with "Dublin Bay". Pressed for his ideal, Dickson said he would like one in orange.

Sam McGredy said that he was trying to produce climbers with flowers from top to bottom and with the majority of flowers carried quite low. In order to achieve this he was working with more shrubby types. I asked him to name his favourite climber, and his reply was "Handel". "Because of its remarkable colouring," I suggested. "No, because of its remarkable ability to generate dollars," he responded.

Sean McCann, author and rose correspondent of *Garden News*, thought climbers were short of publicity, largely because of the dearth of new varieties over the last ten years; apart from "Compassion" and "Dublin Bay" there has been nothing to excite public interest. He grows "Rosy Mantle" and "Grand Hotel" very successfully and is surprised that they are not more popular. He also discussed the possibility of "Eye Paint", a spectacular shrub rose being grown as a climber, but his favourites were two old ones, climbing "Mrs Sam McGredy" and climbing "Ena Harkness". Their nodding blooms were so much more enjoyable than those varieties with stiffer growth that do not permit the viewer a full look at their blooms. When asked what sort of climber he would like to see in the future, he suggested a cross between "Bantry Bay" and "Sexy Rexy".

Surprisingly, Peter Harkness told me that the Harkness nursery had almost stopped breeding specifically for climbers, although it still used climbing pollen.

Climbing roses represent about 9 per cent of its total sales; a figure that was fairly constant. Peter Harkness' own favourite climber is "Compassion": he likes the quality and quantity of bloom, the fragrance, the handsome dark foliage and its adaptability, for it can be grown equally successfully as a shrub. He also particularly likes "White Cockade", which he describes as being leafy right down to the base, healthy and free flowering, and suited to the smaller garden. For the future he thought that gardeners would look for climbers that need the minimum of attention, with not too vigorous growth, no dead-heading, no thorns, a good fragrance and excellent health.

A few years ago Tony Hallows, the hybridist for Bees of Chester, tried to breed improved climbers using mainly "Schoolgirl" and "Handel". Despite hundreds of crosses made each year, he found that most of his seedlings refused to climb. Most were shrubby and in no way an improvement on the two parent roses. He feels that many modern climbers are really nothing but overgrown shrubs, and would like to see a plant similar to "Elegance", which will cover the whole of the side of a house and yet be fully repeat flowering.

Mark Mattock, from Mattocks of Oxford, would like to see new climbers like "Compassion", but in a new assortment of colours, and a new race of repeat-flowering ramblers, which would be climbers with pliant stems that could easily be trained over archways and even along ropes. He visualizes plants with small and quite large flowers. Although large flowers with pliant stems would seem to be impossible, Mattock thought that further developments with the new ground-cover roses could produce these exciting plants. He felt certain that there would be a large public demand for this type of rose because his firm was frequently asked for a repeat-flowering "Dorothy Perkins".

Nan Cocker, Alec Cocker's widow, has still a great affection for "New Dawn" and would like to see more climbers with its growth habit and lovely fragrance. She would love to breed a fragrant red "Silver Jubilee" type plant, and her breeding sights are more strongly set in this direction than on climbers.

Rosemary McCarthy, founder of a new rose firm, Rosemary Roses, says that the public wants fragrant climbing roses above all other qualities, and looks forward to the time when many more of the new repeat-flowering climbers will be blessed also with strong fragrance.

It would appear that little breeding for climbers is going on in the United Kingdom, but fortunately this is not the case in France and Germany with the firms of Delbard-Chabert, Tantau and Kordes. Georges Delbard consistently produces new climbers for the European trials (test gardens) and more often than not is successful. Apart from "Altissimo", none of his creations has reached the United Kingdom. The firm of Tantau has detected an upsurge in public interest in climbing roses and is increasing its efforts to breed new ones. Its most recent release, "Lavinia", is gaining in popularity in the United Kingdom and there are two new ones on the way, one dark red and the other white. Tantau is confident that these both represent a further step forward.

The Kordes firm in Germany has an extensive breeding programme devoted to shrubs, ground covers and climbers as well as its more conventional work. Wilhelm Kordes, great-grandson of the nursery's founder, has told me that the firm makes 5,000 crosses and raises approximately 15,000 seedlings each year in its search for better shrubs and climbers. It is bringing species roses into the programme to get exceptional disease resistance. It is interesting that Kordes believes that *R. kordesii* has not much more to offer. The work with species is bringing the nursery into conflict with many thorns, infertility and once-flowering roses, although the seedlings are healthy and hardy.

Other breeders must be using species in their endeavours to increase the disease resistance of our garden roses, but among the new roses put on the market each year there is not much evidence that great progress has been made. The rose has undoubtedly lost popularity over the last twenty years, and the lack of sufficient disease resistance has undeniably been a reason for this. I would like to see some of the untried species climbers, *R. helenae*, *R. rubus* and *R. sinowilsonii* in particular, used with some of our garden roses.

There is room for more fragrance – only "Compassion" really excels in this respect – among the more recent introductions, and I would love to see more of the synstylae climbers, which cast their fragrance freely into the surrounding air. Perhaps "Veilchenblau" might be a good starting point.

A repeat-flowering rambler would be a welcome addition. How delightful to have a rose like "Dorothy Perkins" with its profusion of bloom, but twice a year instead of once and without the mildew that so readily afflicts "Dorothy Perkins". Surely work with the new ground-covering roses like "Snow Carpet", "Red Bells", "Grouse" and "Partridge" could achieve some exciting results. Nearly all of these new roses have excellent, healthy foliage.

Of course we need more and brighter colours in our new climbers. Imagine a rose as colourful and free flowering as "Trumpeter", not as a 2ft (0.6m) bush, but as a climber, perhaps 10ft (3m) high. Let us add more colours to our climbers – orange, mauve and lilac, brown, deep maroon, vivid scarlet and why not grey or green – and why not hand paints and stripes, which could look stunning against a wall?

Much of my own interest in the last few years seems to have centred on miniature climbers. These happened by chance when I crossed a miniature with a climber and among the seedlings were one or two repeat-flowering miniature climbers. This type of rose ought to have a future in England. Imagine growth a little in excess of 6ft (1.8m) with flowers between 1in (25mm) and 2in (5cm) in diameter produced in bunches from the bottom to the top of the plant. Surely this would have more appeal than a standard rose. Time will tell.

WHITE COCKADE
This fine semi-climber is the best of the short white climbers with its freely borne blooms, attractive foliage and quick repeat flowering. *V. A. Page*

34

Photographed at the Roseraie de l'Hay, Paris, these arches of roses give some idea of the spectacular growth that climbing roses can achieve.
R. C. Balfour

ROSA RUBUS
Sweetly fragrant *R. rubus*
(left) is often most
successfully grown
through a supporting tree.
V. A. Page

**CLIMBING MME.
EDOUARD HERRIOT**
This climbing sport (right)
was introduced in 1921,
and even though the bush
seen here is over seventy
years old, the flowers are
still a stunning colour.
V. A. Page

ROSA BANKSIAE LUTEA
This delightful way of
growing *R. banksiae lutea*
(below left) was
photographed at
Emmerentia, South Africa.
R. C. Balfour

ROSA ANEMONOIDES
Like its more richly
coloured sport "Ramona",
R. anemonoides prefers a
sheltered site. *R. C. Balfour*

ROSARIUM UETERSEN
"Rosarium Uetersen"
(right) is rapidly
establishing itself in
Europe. Its most notable
characteristic is the
number of petals – up to
140 on each flower.
R. C. Balfour

SUMMER WINE
The beautiful display of
stamens of this vigorous
climber (far right) is
enhanced by the delicate
coloration of the petals.
The faintly scented flowers
do not, unfortunately,
appear in profusion.
R. C. Balfour

PARKDIREKTOR RIGGERS
A profusion of strong red flowers is produced amid the glossy dark green foliage, and the repeat flowers almost equal the first in abundance. *V. A. Page*

DORTMUND
A Kordesii climber, "Dortmund" (below left) produces an abundance of single blood red flowers in mid-June and, provided the seed pods are removed, will flower again in September. *V. A. Page*

LEVERKUSEN
This hardy climber (right) produces graceful trusses of lemon-coloured flowers, although the repeat flowers can be slow to appear. *R. C. Balfour*

40

VEILCHENBLAU
Seen from a distance the flowers almost seem blue. "Veilchenblau" should be grown in partial shade, for its delicate colouring will fade in direct sun. *V. A. Page*

THE GARLAND
First raised more than 150 years ago, "The Garland" is still a favourite in many gardens, largely because of its sweet, orange-like fragrance. It is also a very strong grower, achieving heights of 20ft (6.1m) when supported by a tree.
V. A. Page

MEG
Although it will never
produce a great abundance
of blooms, the individual
flowers, which may attain
5in (125mm) in diameter,
are among the most
beautiful of all roses.
R. C. Balfour

ROYAL GOLD
When it is grown in a warm, sheltered spot, "Royal Gold" (far left) will produce large, sumptuously coloured blooms to contrast with its dark, semi-glossy foliage. *V. A. Page*

PAUL'S LEMON PILLAR
Seen here growing against a wall at Mottisfont Abbey, Hampshire, England, the beautifully formed blooms of "Paul's Lemon Pillar" (left) are an unforgettable sight. *V. A. Page*

GLOIRE DE DIJON
Despite its age – it was introduced in 1853 – "Gloire de Dijon" (above) will still perform well and when grown against a wall will often be the first rose to flower. *R. C. Balfour*

MORGENGRUSS
One of the very best of the Kordesii climbers, "Morgengrüss" (below) combines lovely light green foliage with full-petalled pinkish-buff blooms. *W. Kordes*

BANTRY BAY
Free flowering and
producing excellent repeat
blooms, "Bantry Bay" will
continue to produce
flowers until the first frosts.
V. A. Page

DANSE DES SYLPHES
The semi-glossy foliage
(above) is plentiful,
providing a brilliant
contrast with the scarlet
crimson blooms.
V. A. Page

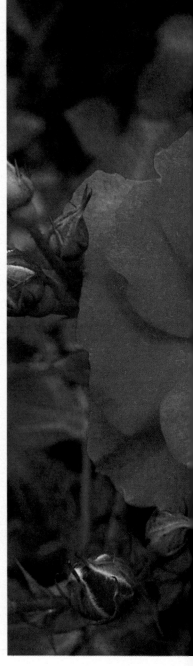

DREAMING SPIRES
Attractive dark green foliage contrasts strongly with the deep yellow blooms of this comparatively recently introduced repeat flowering rose. *R. C. Balfour*

ROSA SINOWILSONII
The magnificent deep red stems, thorns and huge leaves of *R. sinowilsonii* (below left) are among the most exciting foliage of all roses, and, in a mild winter in southern states, the foliage will be retained until the new growth appears in the spring.
Ian Marshall

ROSA KORDESII
Possibly one of the most important roses to be bred this century, *R. kordesii* (below) has excellent foliage and strong resistance to winter cold and produces healthy seedlings. *R. C. Balfour*

51

ROYAL SUNSET
Popular in the United States, "Royal Sunset", with its lovely colouring and fruity fragrance, is not yet widely known in the United Kingdom. It is predominantly upright in habit, and against a wall growth of 10ft (3m) will be achieved. *R. C. Balfour*

SEAGULL
In addition to a profusion of blooms, "Seagull" has a wonderfully sweet scent. It is seen here on a pergola at the headquarters of the Royal National Rose Society at St Albans, England. *V. A. Page*

BLAIRI No.2
Producing a wealth of
large blooms fairly early in
the season, "Blairi No.2"
has a spicy, damask-like
fragrance. *V. A. Page*

KIFTSGATE

"Kiftsgate", a variety of the species *R. filipes*, can achieve heights of 50ft (15.2m) once it is established. The white, single blooms are borne in enormous trusses. *V. A. Page*

ALBERIC BARBIER
The yellow buds open into
clusters of fragrant white
blooms, and some repeat
flowers will appear late in
the season. *V. A. Page*

JOSEPH'S COAT
Although classified as a
semi-climber, "Joseph's
Coat" will reach 8ft (2.4m)
on a supporting wall or
fence. The bright yellow,
orange-tinged flowers,
changing to rich orange
red, will certainly brighten
a dull corner of any
garden. *V. A. Page*

CECILE BRUNNER
The climbing sport of a bush rose, "Cécile Brunner" (far left) has daintily shaped buds that open into symmetrical light pink flowers with a sweet scent. *V. A. Page*

SANDER'S WHITE
A vigorous rambler with strongly scented flowers, "Sander's White" (left) can be trained to almost any situation. *V. A. Page*

SYMPATHIE
A strong grower with very good repeat flowering qualities, "Sympathie" (above) is rather more prone to blackspot than most Kordesii climbers. *R. C. Balfour*

"Paul's Scarlet" and
"American Pillar" seen to
best advantage adorning a
pergola at the Roseraie de
l'Hay, Paris. *R. C. Balfour*

AMERICAN PILLAR
The striking white centre
to the single pink blooms
has undoubtedly been one
of the main reasons for this
climber's great popularity
since it was introduced in
1902. A vigorous grower,
it will reach 20ft (6.1m).
V. A. Page

WESTERLAND
Although often classified as a shrub, "Westerland" (far right) can be grown successfully against a wall or fence. The lovely colouring is complemented by a strong fruity fragrance. *W. Kordes*

PAUL'S HIMALAYAN MUSK
Achieving heights of 30ft (9.1m) or more if grown through a supporting tree, "Paul's Himalayan Musk" deserves to be better known, for its scent is sweet and the double, pale pink flowers are borne in large sprays. *V. A. Page*

MME. GREGOIRE STAECHELIN
Large double blooms with a rich scent are borne in profusion although there are no repeat flowers. It can be grown successfully against a north-facing wall, seen here at Hyde Hall, near Chelmsford, Essex, England. *Above: V. A. Page; right: R. C. Balfour*

FUGUE
"Fugue" (above) bears brightly coloured blooms, which repeat freely.
V. A. Page

RAMONA
One of the loveliest of the single roses, "Ramona" (below) prefers a mild climate or the protection of a warm wall. *R. C. Balfour*

DUBLIN BAY
Although it may take over a year to begin to climb, "Dublin Bay" (above) is the best of the shorter red climbers. *V. A. Page*

LADY HILLINGDON
This sport of the old tea rose (below) requires the protection of a warm south-facing wall.
R. C. Balfour

FRANÇOIS JURANVILLE
Preferred by some to
"Albertine", with which it
is often compared, the
many-petalled flowers (left)
have a delightful fruity
fragrance. It is a strong
grower but does not
produce as much basal
growth as most
Wichuraiana ramblers.
R. C. Balfour

ALLEN CHANDLER
The golden stamens of this
lovely climber (above)
contrast with the deep red
flowers, which, sadly, are
not strongly scented. The
plentiful foliage will
require spraying to keep
blackspot at bay. *R. C. Balfour*

MERMAID
The beautiful golden stamens, for which this vigorous climber is justly famous, remain after the large creamy-yellow petals have fallen. *R. C. Balfour*

ROSA BANKSIAE BANKSIAE
Not generally a free flowering subject, in southern states it is a vigorous climber, and in Arizona a specimen of *R. banksiae banksiae* has grown into the world's largest rose. *R. C. Balfour*

PAUL'S SCARLET
Seen here growing in Seattle, "Paul's Scarlet" was for many years the most popular bright red climbing rose. The abundant vivid red flowers make a wonderful display, and it is one of the first climbers to come into flower. *R. C. Balfour*

SCHOOLGIRL
The excellent form of the orange-yellow, sweetly scented blooms (above) is marred only by the fading of the colour as the flowers open. Against a wall it will grow to 10ft (3m), but the glossy foliage will need to be sprayed to keep blackspot under control.
R. C. Balfour

SPARKLING SCARLET
The outstanding colour and unrestrained growth more than compensate for the lack of petals. Although "Sparkling Scarlet" in the English speaking world, this climber is known as "Iskra" in the rest of Europe. *R. C. Balfour*

NEW DAWN
Although now over fifty years old, this rose's delightful fragrance, shiny foliage and abundant flowers are not matched by many of the more recent introductions. *V. A. Page*

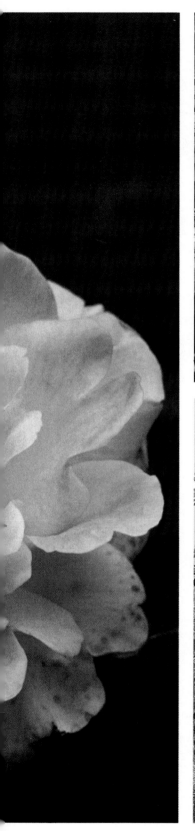

MME. DE SANCY DE PARABERE
Thornless, this is a vigorous and free-flowering variety, which will begin to produce blooms early in the season. *V. A. Page*

MME. ALFRED CARRIERE
More than a hundred years old, but still one of the most popular of all the white climbers. The double flowers (left) are richly fragrant and freely borne. *R. C. Balfour*

KORDISTA
So new that it is not yet commercially available, the orange pink of the petals and profusion of blooms are sure to make "Kordista" (far left) a favourite. *V. A. Page*

73

Heaven on earth – this
beautiful arch of roses was
photographed at Nervi,
Genoa, Italy, where the
park authorities have
initiated new and original
rose trials – the roses are
judged in October on the
basis of how well they have
produced repeat flowers.
R. C. Balfour

CASINO
Best grown in a warm,
sheltered spot, the well
formed yellow buds turn a
softer shade as they open.
V. A. Page

LA MORTOLA
This form of *R. brunonii* (right) appears to be reasonably hardy and, once established, will flower freely and may achieve more than 30ft (9.1m) in height. *V. A. Page*

HANDEL
In hot sun the deep pink of the edges bleaches into the creamy-white of the centre of the flowers (far right). Blooms are produced in great profusion and will continue to appear well into the autumn. *V. A. Page*

ALBERTINE
The freely borne flowers, wonderful copper-pink colour and rich scent have made "Albertine" a great favourite among rose growers for many years. Perhaps its only failing is the rather ragged appearance of the old flowers. *Above: V. A. Page; right: R. C. Balfour*

MORNING JEWEL
Excellent whether growing
over a fence or a short
pillar, "Morning Jewel"
bears semi-double flowers
up to 4in (10cm) across.
R. C. Balfour

ROSA GENTILIANA
The excellent glossy
foliage, freely borne
flowers, strong fragrance
and mass of hips make this
an ideal subject to be
allowed to ramble at will.
R. C. Balfour

LADY BARBARA
Still being tested by several European nurserymen, the tangerine orange blooms and yellow reverse (left) are new in climbing roses.
Ian Marshall

CLAIRE JACQUIER
Although a vigorous grower and generally more hardy than many noisettes, the quantity of repeat flowers is disappointing. *V. A. Page*

GOLDEN RAMBLER
Known in the United Kingdom as "Alister Stella Grey", this slightly tender rose (left) has the form and colouring typical of all noisettes. *V. A. Page*

PINK PERPETUE
This short pillar rose (below) has freedom of flower and quick repeat blooms. *V. A. Page*

ENA HARKNESS
A vigorous climbing sport of the well known hybrid tea, "Ena Harkness" (right) produces repeat flowers exceptionally well. *V. A. Page*

ALOHA
The many-petalled flowers (above and right) open to reveal a pretty terracotta centre. A healthy climber, "Aloha" is equally effective as a hedge or growing against a pillar. *R. C. Balfour*

ALTISSIMO
The large single blooms of "Altissimo" (left) are highlighted by the wonderful display of golden stamens. *V. A. Page*

BLUSH NOISETTE
The probable ancestor of the first repeat-flowering climbing roses, "Blush Noisette" produces almost double, creamy pink blooms. *V. A. Page*

ALEXANDRE GIRAULT
Photographed growing to
perfection at the Roseraie
de l'Hay, Paris, "Alexandre
Girault" can achieve a
height of 20ft (6.1m).
R. C. Balfour

LAWRENCE JOHNSTON
A vigorous grower, suited
to a sheltered wall, the

bright yellow blooms
(above) appear in June.
V. A. Page

ROSA LAEVIGATA
COOPERII
This fine specimen (left)
was photographed in
Madrid, but in cooler
areas, *R. laevigata cooperii*

(''Cooper's Burmese Rose'')
needs a warm wall to
shelter it. *R. C. Balfour*

ZEPHIRINE DROUHIN
Introduced as long ago as
1868, "Zéphirine Drouhin"
is still as lovely as ever. The
beautiful fragrance, freely
borne blooms and good repeat flowering more than
compensate for a tendency
to develop mildew.
R. C. Balfour

PHYLLIS BIDE
A slow-growing rose that will eventually reach a height of 10ft (3m) on a wall, "Phyllis Bide" produces its delicately coloured blooms until quite late in the year.
V. A. Page

PARADE
This reliable and free-flowering rose will tolerate shade. A good crop of the deep pink blooms, up to 4in (10cm) across, is repeated in autumn. *V. A. Page*

EMILY GRAY
The bronzy-yellow flowers
(above) are among the
earliest to appear, and are
complemented by glossy,
almost evergreen foliage.
V. A. Page

DANSE DU FEU
The double orange-scarlet
flowers (left and right) are
borne freely but do not age
gracefully. However,
"Danse du Feu" may be
grown successfully trained
vertically, as here, or
laterally along a wall.
V. A. Page

NOZOMI
A Japanese-bred hybrid,
"Nozomi" (far right) has
dainty flowers and foliage
and a prostrate habit. It
can also be trained to grow
vertically, when it will
achieve a height of 6ft
(1.8m) or more. *R. C. Balfour*

ROSA MULLIGANII
Long wrongly named *R. longicuspis*, *R. mulliganii* (above) is a vigorous scrambler that produces a profusion of blooms.
V. A. Page

MAIGOLD
Sharply thorned, "Maigold" (opposite below) has bronze and yellow blooms and an exotic fragrance. It is seen (left) growing at England's Royal National Rose Society headquarters, St Albans, Hertfordshire.
R. C. Balfour

JOHN CABOT
This Kordesii seedling from Canada obtained a Certificate of Merit in the 1985 Royal National Rose Society trials in England. Although the flowers are on the small side, they are borne in abundance all over the plant. *R. C. Balfour*

GOLDEN SHOWERS
One of the most popular of all climbing roses, "Golden Showers" is hardly ever without blooms during the flowering season. Predominantly an upright grower, it will take several years to exceed 6ft (1.8m). *V. A. Page*

ONE HUNDRED
CLIMBING ROSES

The climbing roses described on the following pages are my
personal selection of what I consider to be
the "best" climbing roses. For convenience, they are grouped
into three sections: species and near relatives; old climbing roses –
i.e., those that were introduced between 1800 and 1921; and modern
climbing roses – i.e., those that have been introduced since 1921.

Species and Near Relatives

Rosa anemonoides

The derivation of the name *R. anemonoides* is something of a mystery, although the flowers do bear some resemblance to the single Japanese anemone. The rose originated with J. C. Schmidt of Erfurt, Germany, in 1895. One of its parents was *R. laevigata*, a near evergreen Chinese species, and the other was an unknown tea rose.

R. anemonoides is a strong growing climber, but it does need the protection of a warm wall; given that, however, there is no reason why it should not be tried in the more northerly areas of the U.S.A. and the U.K. The flowers are quite large, up to 4in (10cm) across, and they are not produced in any great profusion but rather spangle themselves at intervals. They are extremely beautiful, of a soft gentle pink with lighter colouring on the reverse petal. There is some lightening of the colour at the centre of the flower, where the attractively displayed stamens add to the beauty of the flower, darkening at their base to form a red rim. *R. anemonoides* begins to flower fairly early and will provide a show for several weeks. The foliage is perhaps a little sparse, but it is pleasantly glossy although prone to mildew in draughts.

Rosa banksiae banksiae

This form of *R. banksiae* is known also as *albaplena*. It was discovered by William Kerr in a Canton garden and sent to England in 1807, and although it was probably the second of the four Banksiae roses to be sent to England, it was almost certainly the first to flower. It was named after Lady Banks, wife of the President of England's Royal Horticultural Society. *R.b. banksiae* is probably a sport or mutation of the single-flowered form *R.b. normalis* since no plant of *R.b. banksiae* has been discovered growing in the wild. It flowers rather sporadically in the U.S.A., but in southern states and the west coast the blooms provide a sensational billowing mass. Like all Banksiae roses it has a reputation for tenderness but will certainly cope with 23°F (-5°C), possibly even lower, although flowering in the year following a heavy frost will be inhibited.

The double flowers are pure white and rounded, not much more than 1in (25mm) across. It is in flower as early as April in the southern United States and Mediterranean countries, but it is generally well into May before the first flowers appear in the United Kingdom. The plant usually remains attractive for at least nine months, even in frosty areas. The light green, pointed foliage is delightful – profuse, glossy and nearly evergreen – and the flowers have a sweet, penetrating fragrance, reminiscent of violets. Like all Banksiae roses, pruning must be kept to a minimum, with dead wood only being removed, but this, of course, is rarely practicable.

In Tombstone, Arizona, a cutting of Banksiae rooted and, in the favourable climate, thrived. Planted in 1885, it is now the world's largest rose, exceeding 8,000 sq ft (743 sq m), and in April each year millions of white blooms entrance those lucky enough to see and smell them.

Rosa banksiae lutea

Undoubtedly the most popular of the Banksiae roses, *R.b. lutea* flowers far more freely and reliably than other Banksiae in the southern states and the west coast. Although it is tender and needs the protection of a large wall or the support of a large tree, it will, in the right conditions, grow to 30ft (9.1m), so its site must be chosen carefully.

The Royal Horticultural Society sent J. D. Parks to collect this rose from the Calcutta Botanic Garden, which had previously received it from China. It flowered for the first time in England in 1824. Like *R.b. banksiae, R.b. lutea* must be a mutation from one of the original single species because there is no sign of any other rose's characteristics in its make-up. It is one of the first roses of the year to flower, and what a delight those flowers are – about 1in (25mm) in diameter and borne in substantial clusters, they droop and nod most gracefully, with just a hint of scent. The yolky-yellow colour beautifully complements the light green foliage. The stems retain their light green colouring for over a year and the leaves hang on until a really sharp frost. There are no hips because the flowers seem to be completely without any male or female parts. Its natural habit is to grow laterally rather than vertically, and it should be pruned as little as possible because the flowers are produced on sub-laterals, that is, a stem growing from a stem. Ideally, therefore, only dead wood should be pruned.

Rosa bracteata

We have to thank this species for producing one of the loveliest climbers of all – "Mermaid". Although several authorities doubt the stated parentage of "Mermaid" (*R. bracteata* × yellow tea rose), there are many similarities between *R. bracteata* and "Mermaid".

Unfortunately, *R. bracteata* is rather tender and should never be exposed to a freezing wind for any length of time. However, sheltered by a south wall, it will thrive and retain its foliage for most of the year. The flowers, which are quite large, up to 4in (10cm) across, are a beautiful, silky white, and hundreds of prominent yellow stamens add to the flowers' attraction. It has a rich lemon scent.

It thrives in the southern United States and in many countries close to the Mediterranean, but fine specimens may be seen in the United Kingdom at Trelissick in Cornwall and Bicton Gardens in Devon. In a sheltered position *R. bracteata* will grow to 15ft (4.6m), but it is bushy, more often resembling a shrub than a climber. It usually begins to flower shortly after mid-summer and will continue sporadically until early autumn. The dark, dense, shiny green foliage often has nine sets of leaves, and they are unusually rounded rather than pointed at the apex. Thorns are numerous and curved, not ones on which to get caught, while the rounded, slightly hairy hips eventually turn orange.

Rosa brunonii "La Mortola"

The story of *R. brunonii* is a classic example of how a mistake once made is copied by successive authorities until the original error is accepted without question. For many years *R. brunonii* was believed to be the original musk rose: it is very vigorous and has a distinctive musk fragrance, and its vigour and hardiness no doubt contributed to its acceptance as the *R. moschata* that had been brought to Britain, probably during the reign of Elizabeth I. Not until Graham Thomas found a plant of the original *R. moschata* (see page 102) growing at Myddleton House, Enfield, Middlesex, England was the true identity of the musk rose established.

R. brunonii is a rampant grower and profuse flowerer, and it has a powerful fragrance. "La Mortola" is superior even to the original form. Its origin is uncertain: it is known only that Kent nurseryman E. A. Bunyard brought it to England from the famous garden on the Riviera, La Mortola.

"La Mortola", although hardier than most climbers, is recommended only for the warmer parts of the United States and, unless well protected, only the warmer regions of the United Kingdom and Europe. Growth will exceed 30ft (9.1m) in all directions. The clear white flowers are quite large, up to 3in (8cm) across, and are produced in profusion all over the plant. The scent is delightful. The greyish-green leaves are long and pointed and droop beguilingly. The stems hold a stout armoury of curved and hooked thorns – it is not a rose with which to fall out – and the oval hips usually appear in profusion.

Rosa cooperi

R. cooperi is believed to be a hybrid between R. gigantea and probably R. laevigata, but this is by no means certain. Its origins are also uncertain. Some authorities state that it was first grown at the Royal Botanic Gardens, Edinburgh, Scotland, by the curator R. E. Cooper from seed collected in Burma; other authorities claim that the first plant was grown at the then headquarters of the National Rose Society at Haywards Heath, Sussex, England.

Whatever its origins, R. cooperi should thrive in southern Europe and even in southern England. Protected by a warm wall, it may be tried in colder areas. In the right conditions it will grow 30ft (9.1m) in all directions and may, therefore, be classified as a "rampant grower". The attractive foliage is dense, glossy and dark green, and in mild regions it is evergreen. Because the stems are rather stiff for training, it is probably best grown informally into a supporting tree.

The flowers, which are 4in (10cm) across, are more creamy than pure white, going faintly pink with age. They are, as with nearly all species roses, single, but the open flower does show its full beauty with an attractive display of stamens and stigma. Although not particularly profuse, the flowers appear at regular intervals and give the appearance of large butterflies feeding.

Rosa filipes "Kiftsgate"

E. H. Wilson sent R. filipes to England from west China in 1908, but the form "Kiftsgate" seems to have originated from E. A. Bunyard, who probably got it from the Roseraie de l'Hay, on the outskirts of Paris. Bunyard sold a plant to Mrs Muir, who lived at the famous Gloucestershire, England garden Kiftsgate Court, and it is this form, which has proved more vigorous and reliable than the original introduction, that is usually sold by British nurserymen. It is certainly not to be planted in small gardens for it will eventually make anything up to 50ft (15.2m) of growth: in fact, the plant at Kiftsgate Court must now be the largest climbing rose in Britain, having reached a height of 20ft (6.1m) and a spread of 60ft (18.3m).

"Kiftsgate" flowers later than most climbing roses, and it carries enormous heads of bloom on long stems. The single flowers, which are creamy in bud, open white with pronounced stamens and are similar in shape to buttercups. An established plant will provide a cascading sheet of blossom.

"Kiftsgate" is a synstylae rose, and, in common with other roses in that family, casts its sweet scent into the air. The foliage has up to seven leaflets of a dull, almost grey-green. It sets seed very readily, and there is a second display as the small oval hips slowly turn orange in the autumn.

Two fairly recent seedlings from "Kiftsgate" are "Brenda Colvin", which has single, apple-blossom pink flowers, and "Treasure Trove", which has semi-double apricot blooms; both have inherited "Kiftsgate's" vigour.

Rosa gentiliana

Although it is thought by some authorities to be a hybrid between R. multiflora and R. moschata, there are few similarities between R. gentiliana and those two roses, even though it could be argued that R. gentiliana's leaf formation resembles that of R. multiflora and that its flowering truss is of equal proportions. A link with R. sinowilsonii (see page 104) seems possible, for its bright, shiny, deep green foliage, second only to R. sinowilsonii in its lustrous appearance is similar to, although smaller than, that of R. sinowilsonii, and both have red thorns and stems. Introduced by the Frenchman, Bernaix in 1886, *R. gentiliana* is presumed to be a hybrid or a sport because no plant has been found growing wild.

Allowed to ramble into, and cascade from, a tree, *R. gentiliana* should achieve a height of 16ft (4.9m). It seems to be hardier than many species climbing roses and could be tried in Zone 6 of the United States and in most parts of the United Kingdom and Europe. Flowers in large trusses and about 1in (25mm) across, appear in summer only.

The buds are very faintly yellow, opening white with prominent yellow–orange stamens. The abundant flowers and bright foliage are further enhanced by a strong, orange-like fragrance, which is cast freely around. The oval, orange–red hips last well into the winter, making a second show to brighten the duller months.

Rosa gigantea

Seeing *R. gigantea* growing in its native north Burma or south-west China, where it will achieve heights of up to 50ft (15.2m) with flowers as much as 8in (20cm) in diameter, must be an unforgettable experience. In the United States it has a reputation for being tender and is seldom grown, although Bunyard, writing in the 1940s, claimed to have grown it successfully in the open for a number of years.

There appear to be three forms of this rose: two with creamy white flowers and one, "Gigantea Erubescens", with blush- to dark pink flowers. The *R. gigantea* that I grow flowered freely in its fourth year, but its flowers were only some 4in (10cm) across. It is likely that the larger flowered type is the ancestor of the modern large-flowered rose. The foliage is profuse with shiny, very dark green leaves, but beware its thorns, which are curved and very strong. Hips do not seem to be produced in great numbers, although they are attractively elongated, slowly turning from yellow to orange as they ripen.

Rosa helenae

Another member of the synstylae group of roses, *R. helenae* was named after his wife by E. H. Wilson. Although most books give the year of introduction as 1907, it seems probable that it was not growing in England until 1909.

R. helenae is a strong, scrambling grower, achieving heights of up to 20ft (6.1m), but although it is reasonably hardy in most winters in the United Kingdom, a bad season can affect its flowering in the following summer. On the whole this is not a suitable subject for the United States, but southern Europe should be ideal. The flowers, 1½in (4cm) across, are a little larger than those of many of the species climbing roses, and they appear in large bunches spread evenly throughout the plant. More cream than white, the flowers exude a strong fragrance, but the first flowers are not usually out until the beginning of July. The thorns are short but powerful and well hooked, and although the foliage is not especially glossy, it blends well with the flowers. *R. helenae*'s most striking feature is the display made by the bright red hips, which hang in enormous bunches almost as profusely as the berries on a pyracantha.

Rosa kordesii

The story of *R. kordesii* is a tribute to a rose breeder's perseverance in the face of what must have appeared impossible odds. Wilhelm Kordes wanted to breed with a prostrate ground-cover type of rose, "Max Graf", which combines the hardiness, toughness and disease resistance of *R. wichuraiana* and *R. rugosa*. But "Max Graf" was virtually sterile and refused to set any seed. For many years Kordes tried to use it as both a pollen and a seed parent, and eventually two or three hips did set some seed. Only two seedlings were raised, however, of which one turned out to be the rose now known as *R. kordesii*. It was agreed that this rose should be given its name principally to honour its breeder, but in the truest sense of the word it is not a proper species. A species will reproduce itself almost identically from its own self-set seed; the seedlings of *R. kordesii*, which, unlike its parent, proved to be fully fertile, show considerable variation. *R. kordesii* is probably one of the most important roses to have been bred this century, but its full significance is only recently being fully appreciated.

Perhaps more of a shrub than a climber, a free-standing specimen of *R. kordesii* will make about 6ft (1.8m) of growth; against a wall, however, it will comfortably attain 10ft (3m). Opinions differ over whether it is recurrent flowering, but it seems fair to say that it repeats sometimes but not reliably every year. The semi-double flowers are a deep reddish-pink. Some 3in (8cm) across, they are produced all along arching stems. The bright green, glossy foliage, which is extremely tough and disease resistant, is almost more attractive than the flowers. Seed is set very freely, and it is this ability that has proved and is proving of such importance to today's roses, for *R. kordesii* and its offspring offer not only healthier roses that are able to withstand all the fungi which can plague a rose, but also much greater hardiness, thus offering the possibility of roses that can survive the extremes of temperature found in the United States and northern Europe.

Rosa luciae and Rosa wichuraiana

R. luciae and *R. wichuraiana* are very similar in appearance, and for many years there was such confusion between them that it is impossible to say for certain which of the two was used to produce many of this century's most popular ramblers and climbers. They are, however, two quite distinct, very hardy species roses, although available evidence suggests that *R. wichuraiana*, as well as being more vigorous, is the more robust of the two.

R. wichuraiana, which may still be found growing wild in Japan, Korea, eastern China and Taiwan, was introduced to Europe in 1891, although it may have arrived earlier in the United States, where hybrids were marketed from 1897.

The plant is a delight to the eye. Its beautifully polished, near evergreen leaves are dark green and very closely set. There will often be as many as nine leaflets, which are more rounded in form than those of most other species. Although *R. wichuraiana* will make considerable upward growth if allowed to hook itself onto a tree, it is chiefly known as a prostrate ground-covering rose. Because of its lax growth it looks particularly delightful hanging from a tree, where it can be expected to ascend 20ft (6.1m). The single flowers are up to 1½in (4cm) across; quite a bright white, with pronounced, deep yellow stamens, they are sweetly scented. Usually produced in small to medium sized trusses, the flowers do not appear until late summer. Small, dark red hips are freely produced.

R. wichuraiana and *R. luciae* have produced many hybrids, several of which may justly be considered our most important garden roses. Indeed it is likely that there will be more to come, for in addition to its great hardiness *R. wichuraiana* offers rose breeders hope in the fight against blackspot.

Rosa moschata

R. moschata is historically and botanically important because it led to two new races of rose – the damasks and the noisettes – and the noisettes produced the first repeat-flowering climbers. For many years *R. brunonii* was confused with *R. moschata* (see page 99), but the important difference between the two plants is that *R. moschata* flowers later, not at mid-summer. When Graham Thomas budded this rose, his maiden plants produced some flowers, a strong indication of the repeat-flowering characteristic that *R. moschata* had passed on to the 19th-century climbers bred from it.

R. moschata is thought to have originated in Madeira and the countries of the north and south Mediterranean. It is not a particularly beautiful garden plant, having neither attractive foliage nor pretty flowers. Against a wall it will probably attain 10–12ft. Plenty of cream to white flowers are produced in a truss, and they go on appearing until late autumn, possessing the strong and distinctive sweet musk fragrance, but they rather quickly lose their form and flop untidily. The reasonably plentiful foliage is a rather dull dark green.

Rosa mulliganii

There are two other, very similar species to *R. mulliganii* in cultivation, and there may possibly also be hybrids of the three, and this has caused a considerable degree of confusion. For many years *R. mulliganii* has been incorrectly distributed in the United Kingdom as *R. longicuspis*. *R. lucens*, the other similar species, was found by E. H. Wilson in west Szechwan, China, in 1908, and when he sent the seeds to England's Kew Gardens he described them as *R. longicuspis*, later repeating the error with a batch he sent to the Arnold Arboretum.

R. *mulliganii* was raised at the Royal Horticultural Society, Wisley, England from seed collected by George Forrest during his 1917–19 expedition to Yunnan. It was named in honour of Brian Mulligan, then assistant to the Director at Wisley.

In the milder states in winter *R. mulliganii* will retain its foliage longer than most climbers, and in a mild winter it will be evergreen. The new shoots are reddish and will make 20ft (6.1m) of growth in one season. In its second year of growth a shoot will produce a flowering truss from every leaf joint, and one truss will produce anything up to 150 flowers. It is, therefore, one of those roses that must be seen even if you do not have the space to grow it in your own garden. The flowers, which start to appear quite late, usually when other species are finishing, are up to 2in (5cm) across. Single, creamy sometimes nearly white, they have wide-flung yellow stamens, and the fragrance is reminiscent of ripe bananas. The lovely, large-leaved foliage is a deep, shiny green, and though it is not dense, is produced in sufficient quantity to make a plant in full bloom an unforgettable sight. The hips are very small but turn a bright orange–red and can be produced in sufficiently large quantities to make winter visits worth while.

"Ramona" (Rosa anemonoides)

"Ramona" is a sport of *R. anemonoides* (see page 98) and its original parents were probably R. *laevigata* × with a tea rose. The sport occurred on *R. anemonoides* in California in Bietrich and Turner's nursery in 1913. Like *R. anemonoides*, "Ramona" is a slightly tender rose, and although it will flourish in the open in the milder states, it does need the protection of a warm wall in colder districts.

The single flowers are quite beautiful: 4in (10cm) across and a vibrant red-pink on the upper surface with a much paler pink, almost grey reverse. The colour all but disappears at the petal centre and the combination of this with the many stamens is an unforgettable sight. There are occasionally a few additional blooms late in the season.

Rosa rubus

Although it is not particularly well known, *R. rubus* is an even more vigorous climber than *R. helenae* (see page 101), which it resembles. There seem to be two forms in cultivation, one with smooth stems, the other with down on most of the growth. The smooth-stemmed form is a more attractive garden plant.

R. *rubus* is reasonably hardy in Zone 6 but is not suitable for the harder climates of northern Europe. Best grown through the branches of a supporting tree, it should eventually reach 20ft (6.1m) or more. The flowers, which are 1½in (4cm) across and are produced at mid-summer, open white, but the bright yellow stamens, with a hint of yellow at the base of the petals, produce a stronger overall colour than most of the species climbers. The large flowering trusses, which bear thirty to forty blooms on each stem, have a very sweet, *R. multiflora* scent. Reginald Farrer, coming across the rose in China, described the air as being "drunk with its sweetness".

The stems have large, curved thorns, and the pleasantly glossy foliage, slightly purplish on the underside when young, has a noticeably toothed edge. Small, dark red hips are produced in abundance. In view of its many good qualities, it is rather surprising that no forms suitable for the average garden have been developed.

Rosa sinowilsonii

In a mild winter *R. sinowilsonii* will retain its foliage until the new growth starts in the spring, so the plant is worth looking at the whole year through. Discovered by E. H. Wilson, hence the name which the rose now bears, it did not reach Britain until this century.

R. sinowilsonii has a reputation for being somewhat tender, and it probably should not be attempted in northern areas of the United Kingdom unless in a warm, sheltered site. It is a rampant grower and will certainly make 15ft (4.6m) of growth in one season when established. The pretty white flowers grow in medium sized clusters and have a pleasant, orange-like scent. The new growth is a most attractive reddish-brown – a colour the plant retains for most of the season. The thorns, which are reddish-brown also, are curved. The leaves have the same attractive colouring on the underside, but the upper leaf is a wonderful deep, lustrous green with deeply toothed incisions. A mature plant will develop leaves anything up to 12in (30cm) in length. The medium sized hips are rounded and take a long time to change colour, eventually becoming pale orange.

There is only one known hybrid of this rose, "Wedding Day", which was raised by Sir Frederick Stern at Highdown, Sussex, England in 1950, and it is somewhat surprising that more efforts have not been made to hybridize from this species since, apart from its fine foliage and rampant growth, it is possibly totally immune to disease.

OLD CLIMBING ROSES : 1800 – 1921

"Aimée Vibert"

"Aimée Vibert" is said to be a cross between a noisette and a *R. sempervirens* hybrid, and nearly all books give its date of introduction as 1828. It seems likely, however, that the original introduction resembled a shrub and that this shrub sported to a more vigorous plant, which was introduced by Curtis in 1841. Thus it is probably not true that "Aimée Vibert" was the first ever repeat-flowering climbing rose.

The form of "Aimée Vibert" that we grow today will achieve a height of anything up to 15ft (4.6m) in an environment that suits it. It is, however, slightly tender and needs the protection of a wall in the milder states, although it should cope with a more open situation in southern Europe. *R. sempervirens*, which originated in southern Europe and north Africa, is almost evergreen, and it is probably because of this that "Aimée Vibert" has more attractive foliage than any other rose in the noisette group. The very deep green, elongated and shiny leaves are beautifully displayed on the branch, and the flowers appear on its basal tips so that an even spread of bloom is produced. The buds are a very pale pink, but the open flowers are white, with a display of yellow stamens.

In a protected environment it may be expected to flower all season long, and its later flowering is often superior to the first, especially if the preceding winter has caused some damage. There is a scent, but not a significantly pleasant one, Graham Thomas considers it the finest of the white repeat-flowering ramblers.

"Albéric Barbier"

I once saw a fence 30ft (9.1m) long and 5ft (1.5m) or so high completely smothered with this rose. There did not seem to be a single space where flowers were not be seen. It was a spectacular sight and a memory to be treasured.

"Albéric Barbier" was raised by the firm of the same name at Orleans, France. It was marketed in 1900 and is a result of a cross between *R. wichuraiana* and "Shirley Hibberd", a yellow tea rose. Predominantly a lateral grower, it is most effective trained sideways rather than upwards. It seems to be hardy enough to cope with all British weather conditions, and will ultimately grow to more than 20ft (6.1m). The rich, dark green leaves are very glossy and profuse and are produced from top to bottom of the plant; they appear to be highly resistant to blackspot. Moreover, since it is nearly evergreen, it retains its beauty late in the year. Flowers appear distinctly yellow in the bud, but as they expand, this colour softens to a rich cream, although there is still some yellow towards the centre of the petals. The newly opened blooms are often pleasantly quartered, but the older flowers can look bedraggled. The rather refreshing green apple fragrance is strong enough to make you linger for a second sniff. The first flowers generally appear before mid-summer and last for about three weeks. Late in the autumn a scattering of blooms will appear. "Albéric Barbier" does not appear to produce hips and is presumably infertile; nothing has been bred from it.

"Albertine"

Although this is the best known of all ramblers, it is perhaps surprising that a rose that has only three weeks of bloom should have remained so long a favourite. Its ability to strike readily from cuttings is part of the reason for its popularity, as is its constant production of new shoots from the base, so that no matter how it is grown the plant is always well covered with foliage.

"Albertine" was bred by Barbier, 21 years after "Albéric Barbier" first appeared. It is the result of a cross between *R. wichuraiana* and

"Mrs A. R. Waddell", a hybrid tea. With support, this rose will easily reach 20ft (6.1m), but it perhaps looks at its best as a huge, shrubby mound. However, so pliant in growth is it, that it can be trained to almost any situation. Foliage is plentiful, reddish when new, eventually turning a pleasant mid-green. Unfortunately, it is prone to mildew, and spraying or regular watering may be necessary. From red-tinted buds, the flowers open a glorious shade of coppery-pink. This colouring has never quite been recaptured in any other rose, and for this quality alone we should revere "Albertine". The expanded flowers are something of a glorious muddle, covering the plant from top to bottom. They are sweetly fragrant and cast their scent into the air around, particularly on warm summer evenings. "Albertine" is very thorny, but it can be quite savagely pruned to any shape required. To date, nothing of worth has been bred from it.

"Alexandre Girault"

This rose is the star of the Roseraie de l'Hay, where approximately eighty plants of "Alexandre Girault" cover a large domed arbour and screen, presenting an unforgettable mass of bloom. Introduced in 1909, it is another of Barbier's creations, this one from a cross between *R. wichuraiana* and "Papa Gontier", a deep pink China rose, which was popular as a cut flower in days long gone even at the end of the 19th century.

Growth of up to 20ft (6.1m) in all directions is possible, especially with support, but it is very much a lateral grower and could even be used for ground cover. It is a mid-season rose, producing flowers in small trusses, but in enormous profusion over the whole plant. The medium sized flowers, which have a sweet, fruity fragrance, are full of petals so that the effect of the open flower is rather muddled. The plant tends to look better from a distance when the overall colour impression is of deep pink, although closer inspection reveals some orange-yellow at the base of each petal. The profuse, glossy foliage is a light green that turns darker. It has a good reputation for disease resistance.

"Golden Rambler"

This rose was raised by an amateur, A. H. Gray of Bath, Somerset, England and it was introduced by G. Paul & Son in 1894. Unfortunately, we do not know its parentage, but its characteristics suggest that it was a noisette crossed with a yellow tea rose. It is known as "Alister Stella Gray" in the U.K.

Although of only average vigour, "Golden Rambler" will make shoots 8ft (2.4m) long in one season, and being of more upright than lateral habit, it will eventually reach a height of about 15ft (4.6m) if protected and supported by a wall. The new growth has smooth, green bark, which does not lose its colour until quite late in the season, but there are a few irregularly placed thorns. The mid-green foliage is not particularly glossy nor is it dense, although it adequately clothes the plant. It is generally, in mild climates in flower by mid-June and should have a fair covering of blooms before the end of the month. The buds, which seem to hold their form for longer than most climbing roses, are buff-yellow in the early stages, opening somewhat paler but with a darker centre. The double flowers, 2½in (6cm) across, are pleasantly quartered and are usually produced in medium sized trusses. The autumn growth is both more thorny and more floriferous, and September's flowering will often be superior to that earlier in the year. It is pleasantly but not strongly scented, with a fragrance, part musky, part tea, that is difficult to define.

"American Pillar"

An old favourite on both sides of the Atlantic, "American Pillar" is stocked by nurserymen nearly ninety years after its introduction. Introduced in 1902 by Dr W. van Fleet, the American breeder responsible for a wide range of important climbing roses, it has an interesting parentage: (R. wichuraiana × R. setigera) × unnamed red hybrid perpetual. R. setigera is an American species rose, found growing wild in the eastern prairies, that will attain heights of 6ft (1.8m) or more if near support.

"American Pillar" is very vigorous, reaching 15–20ft (4.6–6.1m), and it will throw strong, thorny, weeping shoots during one season's growth. It is easily trained, but the old wood must be removed right down to the base after each flowering if it is to give of its best the following season. This can be an irksome task, particularly if it is grown into a supporting tree. The foliage is plentiful, a bright glossy, dark green, which ages to a darker hue as the season progresses. Mildew may appear on the foliage in a dry season, but generally "American Pillar" is much more resistant than most of this type. The blooms do not appear until summer, but then, for three or four weeks, there is a magnificent display; unfortunately, there are no flowers later in the season. The single flowers, 2½in (6cm) across, are a bright glowing pink with a white centre, the contrast between the pink petal and white centre being the distinctive feature of this rose. If left unpruned, "American Pillar" will produce a clutch of hips, but this will, of course, impair the following season's flowering.

"Blairi No. 2"

We know that "Blairi No. 2" was introduced in 1845 by an Englishman, Blair, but there is no recorded parentage. It is assumed that it is of bourbon origin. Predominantly upright in habit, it will exceed a height of 12ft (3.7m) on a wall. The foliage has been described as rather coarse, but I find it plentiful, light green and satisfying. In the south of England the first flowers appear in early June, and soon the whole plant is smothered in bloom. The flowers usually appear in trusses of three, about 4in (10cm) across, very full, often quartered. They are predominantly deep pink, but there is a mauvish-purple centre and the expanded flower shows an attractive and unusual pale, almost white, rim. There is a deep, spicy, damask-like fragrance. Although "Blairi No. 2" has only one main flush of bloom, there are occasional additions throughout the remainder of the season.

"Blush Noisette"

The original noisette rose is extremely important as it led to a whole new race of repeat-flowering climbing roses, the only repeat-flowering climbers for very many years. However, there is some confusion about the parentage of "Blush Noisette". It is known that John Champney, the owner of a large plantation garden near Charleston, South Carolina, grew the musk rose *R. moschata* and "Old Blush China", and that "Champney's Pink Cluster" arose from a cross between the two *c.*1802. It was long believed that seeds collected from this rose gave rise to "Blush Noisette", which was originated in 1813–14 by Philippe Noisette, a French nurseryman living in Charleston. Because of the characteristics of "Blush Noisette", American researcher Léonie Bell has suggested that Champney's rose was cross-pollinated with another newcomer of the time, "Hume's Blush Tea-scented China". The truth will probably never be known, but no doubt the speculation will continue.

Grown as a shrub, "Blush Noisette" will make 5–6ft (1.5–1.8m) of growth; supported by a wall it will achieve up to 12ft (3.7m). The plentiful, fairly large foliage, which covers the plant from top to bottom, is mid-green, and although it is not glossy, it complements the flowers. The stems are nearly thornless, and the new growth is deep red. The many-petalled flowers, which are borne continuously from mid-summer onwards in large sprays, are deep pink in bud, lighter on opening and fading paler still. There is a penetrating, spicy fragrance.

"Cécile Brunner"

The bush rose, "Cécile Brunner", the result of a cross between a dwarf *R. multiflora* hybrid and a pink tea rose, "Mme. de Tartas", was introduced by Frenchman Veuve Ducher in 1881. The climbing sport was discovered in 1894 by the American, F. P. Hosp. No doubt the *R. multiflora* ancestry has contributed to the vigour of this rose, which will ultimately make 20ft (6.1m) across and as much upwards. The climbing sport is generally considered a superior plant to the bush form, for it has larger foliage and at peak flowering is a mass of bloom.

Flowering begins around May in the southern states and will last for several weeks. After the main flush is over, blooms are produced sporadically for the rest of the season but never in any quantity. The little flowers are delightfully shaped, with a dainty, long bud and an open flower that retains its symmetry, the petals neatly arranged from the flower centre. The blooms are a clear, light pink, slightly deeper in the centre, and very few exceed 1½in (4cm) across. In fact, apart from the size of the foliage, it could almost be called a climbing miniature. It has a pleasant, sweet fragrance.

This rose is occasionally wrongly called climbing "Bloomfield Abundance".

"Claire Jacquier"

Raised by a Frenchman, A. Bernaix, and introduced in 1888, "Claire Jacquier" is similar in appearance to "Alister Stella Gray", but while "Alister" scores with better repeat bloom, "Claire Jacquier" is more vigorous and hardier. On a wall it will exceed 20ft (6.1m), possibly even reaching 30ft (9.1m). The profuse and attractive foliage is a glossy bright green. The sweetly scented flowers, which are produced in small trusses, usually appear early in the season. They are attractively shaped in the bud, but rather untidy when fully open. The overall impression is of a creamy-yellow, but with a much deeper apricot-yellow centre. Sadly, this colouring soon disappears in the open flowers, which revert to cream. There is a big crop at the first flowering, and a large plant in full bloom is a wonderful sight. Probably because of its extra vigour, the repeat bloom tends to be spasmodic, and only occasional later flowers can be expected.

"Desprez à Fleur Jaune"

Raised by R. Desprez of Yebles, France, in 1830, "Desprez à Fleur Jaune" is quite possibly one of the oldest surviving repeat-flowering climbing roses. It is reputed to be a hybrid between "Blush Noisette" and "Park's Yellow Tea-scented China".

Very few nurserymen stock this rose, which

is known also as "Jaune Desprez", and we have to thank Graham Thomas for reviving interest in it. If it is to achieve its full potential, it should be grown against a warm wall, and it is not recommended for a cold site. In the right situation it is one of those roses that is rarely without a bloom, and it should flower from early summer until the first frosts. It can make 15–20ft (4.6–6.1m) of growth up a wall. The fully double flowers are not large, only 2in (5cm) across, and they are a blend of gentle shades of yellow-apricot and peach. The flower form is flat and quartered, and the newly opened petals have an appealing freshness. The strong and unusual scent is redolent of ripe bananas.

"Devoniensis"

As far as I know, "Devoniensis" is the only commercially available climbing rose to have originated in Devon. There seems, however, to be some doubt about its true origin. Climbing "Devoniensis" is a sport from an original bush form, which is recorded in 1838 as a cross between "Smith's Yellow" and "Park's Yellow Tea-scented China". In 1841 a nurseryman from Exeter, Devon, introduced the rose and almost certainly gave it its name, and in 1858 the bush form sported into a climber. As *R. gigantea* appears in the parentage of "Park's Yellow Tea-scented China", it is not surprising that bush plants descended from it occasionally throw long climbing shoots.

Climbing "Devoniensis" is a tender rose and can be recommended only for mild districts and warm walls. It will climb 12ft (3.7m) and will produce flowers over a long period although rarely in much profusion. It has a mass of intricately folded, predominantly creamy petals that have a deeper, near apricot, centre. The foliage is rather limp, but there is a rich tea scent. It is known also as the Magnolia rose.

"Emily Gray"

A cross between "Jersey Beauty" and "Comtesse du Cayla", "Emily Gray" was raised in England by Dr A. H. Williams and introduced in 1918. "Jersey Beauty" arose from a *R. wichuraiana* cross, and many of the characteristics of "Emily Gray" may be traced to its species ancestry. "Comtesse du Cayla" was a China rose of good scent and strong flame colouring.

Although it is reasonably hardy in the United Kingdom, reports from the United States suggest that "Emily Gray" is reliable only in the south. Protected by a wall, it will attain 20ft (6.1m), the new growth being a deep, shiny bronze, particularly beautiful when the early and late sun strikes it. Eventually the bronze turns to a deep green, but the foliage remains an attractive and distinctive feature of this rose and often lasts well into the winter. The first flowers appear usually before mid-summer and in small trusses liberally spread throughout the plant. They are a delightful rich buff-yellow, a colour not recaptured to this day in any modern climber. The blooms are a little over 2in (5cm) across, and there is only a double row of petals, but the stamens make a pronounced display when the bloom is fully expanded. Fragrance is strong but, sadly, after about four weeks there are rarely any more blooms. This rose may be badly affected by mildew in a dry situation, so keep it well watered.

"Emily Gray" is one of the few climbers to receive a gold medal from England's National Rose Society; it received this honour in 1916.

"Félicité et Perpétué"

Do not be deceived by the name of this rose: it is not perpetual flowering, in fact it has but a three or four week burst of bloom. Despite its relatively short flowering period, however, it has remained one of the most popular ramblers.

It was raised in 1827 by A. A. Jacques of France and is believed to be a *R. sempervirens* hybrid, but the other parent is unknown. That parent must have been a hardy rose, however, because "Félicité et Perpétué" is grown in all parts of the United Kingdom. The rose was named after Jacques' two daughters, who had been named to commemorate two Christian martyrs.

A very strong grower, achieving heights up

to 20ft (6.1m), this is a very adaptable rose, which can be used in almost any situation. The dark, shiny foliage is nicely in proportion to the flowers, and in mild winters it will remain on the plant for much of the year. The flowers, carried on long stems usually some way above the foliage, are produced quite late in the season. At peak flowering, the whole plant can be covered in bloom. Light pink buds open to cream-white, many-petalled flowers, 1½in (4cm) across, which display near perfect symmetry. It has a light, pleasant fragrance.

"La Follette"

This is not a rose for the average garden. A hybrid of *R. gigantea*, it is extremely vigorous but sadly will not survive in any other than a mild climate. It can be recommended only for southern and milder western States and for southern Europe. In the United Kingdom it is possible to grow it outdoors only in a well-sheltered and protected environment in the south. It has been grown successfully in the United Kingdom, but only under glass: there is a superb plant at Southhill Park, Bedfordshire, which has grown to cover an area 50 × 30ft (15 × 9m) and which produces nearly two thousand blooms during the spring months.

"La Follette" was raised *c.*1910 at Cannes in the south of France. We know that one parent was *R. gigantea*, but the other was not recorded. It will attain 20ft (6.1m) and more in a favourable environment. The buds are long and elegant, with a deep coppery-pink reverse. When open, the large flowers are a pleasant shade of rich rose-pink with plenty of petals and a fairly lax form. It is nicely scented, profuse in flowering but there is rarely any repeat flower. Flowering begins two or three weeks before the longest day, much earlier under glass.

"François Juranville"

"François Juranville" was raised by Barbier and introduced in 1906, being a cross between *R. wichuraiana* and "Mme. Laurette Messimy", a bright salmon-pink China rose, clearly responsible for the climber's colouring.

"François Juranville" is a very strong grower, achieving heights up to 25ft (7.6m), but it does not produce as much basal growth as most of the Wichuraiana ramblers, so there is a risk of it looking rather bare at the base, a fault that may be overcome by the hard pruning back of one of the main shoots.

The glossy foliage is typical of Wichuraiana roses, and the new growth has a bronzy look. Flowers begin early in the U.K., continuing with an abundant display well into July. The many-petalled flowers are a pretty salmon-pink, and from afar the plant looks spectacular. Close inspection of the individual blooms, however, may be disappointing as the petals give the appearance of fighting for the available space. It has a delightful, sweet and fruity fragrance, for which most growers forgive its untidy blooms. As with "Albéric Barbier" there are usually some more blooms later in the season. It will not flourish with dry roots, mildew being a problem, and unless you are prepared to water it, avoid planting it against walls that do not receive the prevailing rainfall.

"The Garland"

Of all the old climbing roses "The Garland" is the only species by species cross to gain a place as a garden rose. It was raised by Wells in 1835, and W. Paul announced that it was a cross between *R. moschata* and *R. multiflora*. Although it has several characteristics that may be seen in these two species, the fact that the petalage is semi-double (rather than single) does raise at least one question.

"The Garland" is a very strong grower and is reputed to be one of the quickest to clothe a pillar. Wending its way into a supporting tree, growth up to 20ft (6.1m) can be expected. The dark green foliage is half-way between matt and glossy, but the green bark and very dark thorns are distinctive. Flowers appear in England towards the end of June, and it is fairly quickly in full flower, although spent by the end of July. There are no repeat blooms, but the great profusion of flowers is a compensation. The pinkish buds open to creamy-white flowers that are so flat that the yellow stamens appear to be very prominent. The firm stems tend to turn the flowers skywards, and it is perhaps best to let this rose grow as a large sprawling bush. One of the reasons for its continuing popularity is undoubtedly the sweet, rather penetrating fragrance of honey and oranges. At the end of the season small red hips are produced in profusion.

"Gloire de Dijon"

Raised by Jacotot of Dijon, France, introduced in 1853 and still going well, "Gloire de Dijon" is one of the most famous roses of all time. If you are ordering a new plant, choose carefully because some inferior plants are put on the market. Ideally go and see the plants growing in a nurseryman's fields.

"Gloire de Dijon" is the result of a cross between an unknown tea rose and a bourbon "Souvenir de la Malmaison". Why this particular parentage should have produced such a vigorous rose is a mystery, unless, of course, the unknown tea was closely linked to R. gigantea. In full flower this rose is a glorious sight. The flowers, each about 4in (10cm) across, are packed with petals, often quartered, sometimes rather a muddle, and it is a subtle blend of apricot, buff and peach. All reports speak of its strong fragrance, although it can vary according to the weather conditions.

This rose is completely hardy in all Zone 6 areas. It can, with age, become a little bare at the base, so it is probably better planted with something else in front of it.

"Lady Hillingdon"

Climbing "Lady Hillingdon" is a sport of a bush tea rose, and it is another of those roses with unique colouring that has been approached but never recaptured by modern roses. The bush was introduced in 1910 by Lowe and Shawyer and was the result of a cross between two tea roses, "Papa Gontier" and "Mme. Heste". The climbing sport was introduced in 1917.

Although of doubtful hardiness, this rose thrives in many gardens in milder states, and it could reasonably be tried further north in adequately protected surroundings, a warm south wall being ideal. It is surprisingly vigorous and should comfortably attain 15ft (4.6m). The new growth is a delightful copper-beech shade, which is retained until the season is well advanced, eventually turning a deep green. The leaves have a degree of glossiness and, although by modern standards they could be deemed sparse, contribute to the grace and airiness of the plant. The flowers, produced early and continuing spasmodically very late in the season, often until the first frosts, are borne on soft flower stems (pedicles), which cause the flowers to nod so that the viewer from below sees them to perfection. The blooms are a rich but gentle shade of apricot-orange, with a stronger colour on the surface of the inner petal, so that the impression is one of colour deepening towards the flower centre. There are plenty of petals, and the flower form resembles that of today's hybrid teas. It has an unusual and quite powerful tea scent, which is intriguing and puzzling at the same time.

"Lawrence Johnston"

This rose was raised in 1923 from a cross between "Mme. Eugene Verdier" and R. foetida persiana, but preferring its sister seedling, "La Rêve", French hybridist Pernet-Ducher did not bother to market the rose. Major Lawrence Johnston bought the only plant and transferred it to his garden at Hidcote in Gloucestershire, England. Several years later Graham Thomas saw the rose and asked if he could exhibit it: Major Johnson agreed, asking only that it be named after him. It quickly gained recognition, winning England's Royal Horticultural Society's award of merit in 1948 and an 8.0 rating from the American Rose Society as recently as 1979.

"Lawrence Johnston" is a very strong grower, achieving heights in excess of 20ft (6.1m), and it will have a profusion of spring bloom. After the first flush is over, occasional blooms are produced for the remainder of the season but never in any quantity. The foliage, a bright, shiny green, is a very satisfactory complement to the bright yellow flowers, which retain much of their depth of colour until the petals are about to fall.

The flowers appear rather loose when the petals are expanded, but the wealth of bloom more than compensates for any lack of quality in the individual blooms. There is a strong scent.

"Mme. Alfred Carrière"

Who could forget the sight of this rose growing on the wall of the cottage at Sissinghurst, Kent, England? The whole front wall of the cottage is covered, and there scarcely seems a space where blooms are not appearing. It was raised by the French grower J. Schwartz and introduced in 1879. The records of its parentage are not extant, but it has characteristics of both noisette and tea roses. One parent was probably fairly hardy, because it does seem to be tougher than most of the noisettes.

Against a wall it will grow to 20ft (6.1m), and although it is predominantly an upright grower, it is sufficiently pliant to be trained sideways without much difficulty. The new growth is a bright shade of green with plentiful foliage and with very few thorns. It retains this appearance until quite late in the season. An established plant will be in almost constant flower production, with occasional flowers between two main periods. Flowering starts in June, reaching a peak at the beginning of July. Another flush may be expected in September. Faintly pink buds open to quite large flowers that are initially creamy but fairly quickly turn white. There are many petals, which contribute to the hybrid tea form of the bud, but the open flower is usually muddled or quartered. There is a sweet scent.

"Mme. Caroline Testout"

The bush rose "Mme. Caroline Testout" was raised in 1890 by French hybridist J. Pernet-Ducher from a cross between "Mme. de Tartas" and "Lady Mary Fitzwilliam". The climbing sport was discovered by Chauvry in 1901 and introduced in 1902, fairly quickly becoming a British favourite. One of the main reasons for its popularity was its willingness to produce further flowers after the main crop, for many of the climbing sports are unreliable, only rarely having any repeat bloom and even the main flowering can be disappointingly sparse.

At least 15ft (4.6m) of growth can be expected. It is an upright grower, but, because it branches fairly freely from the main stems, it does not present too many problems in training, although thorns are plentiful. Not dense by today's standards, the foliage is a mid-green, rather dull colour. It is a mid-season rose, with flowers that are large, full and globular. The colour, although always in shades of rose-pink, is rather variable and can appear harsh and unattractive; it is not, therefore, to everyone's taste. I cannot detect much scent, but Peter Beales writes of a strong fragrance. After a heavy first crop, flowers are produced almost continuously, but never abundantly, until the first frosts.

"Mme. Edouard Herriot"

The British newspaper, the *Daily Mail*, organized a competition for a new seedling rose, and the eventual winner was the rose that bears the dual title of the "Daily Mail" rose and "Mme. Edouard Herriot". The rose, which was named in 1913, was raised by Pernet-Ducher, and it was the result of a cross between "Mme. Caroline Testout" and an unnamed hybrid tea. The latter undoubtedly possessed the genes of "Persian Yellow", for "Mme. Edouard Herriot" set new standards of both colour and flamboyance.

The climbing sport was introduced in 1921 by the Ketten brothers, nurserymen from Luxemburg. It is more restrained than most of this type but will reach 10ft (3m) with support. Growth is upright, but it can be trained sideways if the new growth is tied into position before it has hardened. The medium sized flowers have over twenty petals and are, initially, very striking, being a bright terracotta red with some yellow and scarlet shades. When first in flower it is a wonderful sight, the blooms hanging their heads to the onlooker. Sadly, the vivid colouring rapidly fades to a crushed strawberry. It has a pleasant fragrance, but after the first impressive flush of flower not very many repeat blooms appear. The attractive glossy bronze foliage is liable to blackspot in troublesome areas.

"Mme. de Sancy de Parabère"

This rose belongs to a small group called boursault roses, which are distinguished by smooth, thornless stems, very dark wood and a typical leaf form. Their origin is uncertain, and all that is known for certain is that "Mme. de Sancy de Parabère" originated in the nursery of A. Bonnet in France c.1870. At Mottisfont "Mme. de Sancy" has reached a lateral spread of 15ft (4.6m) and is up to 10ft (3m) high. The plentiful foliage is a matt dark green. Flowering begins early in the season and for a three to four week period the plant will be a picture. Crowds of petals eventually settle into a more or less symmetrical pattern, with those in the centre held tight and the other petals spreading ever wider, until a bloom up to 5in (13cm) across is reached. Most authorities describe the colouring as rich pink, but a positive mauvy cast to the shade may be detected. The scent is gently pleasant.

"Maréchal Niel"

How the rose world rejoiced at the appearance of this rose: here at last was a real yellow to add to the pinks, creams, whites and reds already in cultivation. It remained a favourite in the United Kingdom for over forty years and would undoubtedly be a favourite to this day but for one fatal weakness – "Maréchal Niel" is not hardy out of doors except in very mild regions of the United Kingdom, Mediterranean countries and the southern and Pacific States.

It was raised by Henri Pradel and introduced in 1864. No one is sure of the parentage, but the noisette "Chromatella" is a possibility as is "Isabella Gray". Yellow has always presented problems to rose breeders, and even today there is not an entirely satisfactory yellow rose.

In mild climates "Maréchal Niel" may be expected to reach 15ft (4.6m). The foliage is light green and fairly glossy but not dense. Flowering is more or less continuous, but a mass of bloom cannot be expected except in warm climates. The flowers are full, medium to large, and a soft yellow with some apricot. The flowers nod gracefully to the onlooker but quickly look untidy in wet conditions. It has a pronounced "tea rose" scent, an aroma similar to the one experienced when a packet of tea is freshly opened.

"Maréchal Niel" may be grown successfully under glass, but the roots must be outside, otherwise growth will be disappointing.

"Mermaid"

Most experts say that it is impossible to breed a perpetual-flowering rose from a species rose because the once-flowering genes are dominant, and the dominance is not usually broken until at least two generations of parent have been used. There is, therefore, some controversy surrounding the parentage of "Mermaid", but as the raiser, William Paul of Hertfordshire, England, was an experienced nurseryman and rose breeder, it seems highly unlikely that he made a mistake and wrongly recorded the parentage – R. bracteata and an unnamed double yellow tea rose. "Mermaid" won a gold medal in 1917 from the National Rose Society and was introduced in 1918.

"Mermaid" is tender, but it is worth all the protection it can be given. Once it has settled down, which may well take two years, it is a very strong grower. Its huge, arching, thorny growth will comfortably reach 20ft (6.1m), quite possibly 30ft (9.1m). Its narrow foliage, glossy and profuse, is distinctive and very resistant, although not completely immune, to disease. It is virtually evergreen in a mild winter. The flowers are large, 5in (13cm) across, and single, but the pale primrose colour is greatly enhanced by a boss of wide-flung, deep yellow stamens. The petals are short lived, but the memory lingers for the stamens remain for two or three days more. "Mermaid" is never a mass of bloom, but it produces flowers with scarcely a break until the frosts, and it is often particularly free flowering in the autumn. It must always be handled with care, for in addition to its vicious hooked thorns, its long stems must be trained early as they are very brittle. It is often said to be sterile, and indeed only rarely does it produce any seed, but pollen is there if it is caught sufficiently early.

"Paul's Himalayan Musk"

Originating in the Hertfordshire, England nursery of William Paul towards the end of the last century, "Paul's Himalayan Musk" has the fragrance of *R. multiflora* and drooping leaves of *R. moschata*, but there is more colour in the flowers than either of these species possesses, and it seems likely that a pink hybrid was involved in its parentage.

This rose is a mighty scrambler, and allowed to hook its way into a supporting tree, it is likely to exceed 30ft (9.1m) with pliant stems spreading freely in all directions. The semi-glossy, pointed and slightly drooping foliage is plentiful. It is not usually in flower until after midsummer, when large sprays will hang down on slender stems. The double flowers, small, blush pink with lilac undertones, possess a sweet multiflora scent, which is cast freely into the air.

"Paul's Lemon Pillar"

"Paul's Lemon Pillar" appeared two years before "Mermaid" and gained a gold medal from England's National Rose Society in 1915. Although only once flowering. "Paul's Lemon Pillar" remained popular until after World War II, and it is still unsurpassed in its colour range for quality of bloom.

It is a cross between "Frau Karl Druschki" and "Maréchal Niel", and although one would suspect that it might be a little tender with "Maréchal Niel" as one parent, it seems to thrive in all but cold or very exposed situations. Protected by a wall, it can be expected to reach 20ft (6.1m). It has large but rather dull, midgreen foliage. The spring blooms continue for several weeks. The flowers are of nearexhibition quality in form, but the nodding stems, which allow the observer at ground level to see them to perfection, usually keep the rose from the show bench. There is little lemon in the colouring, except in the early stages. The overall impression is of milky whiteness with a noticeable greenish tint at the centre of the flower. The petals curl back at their extremities, almost as though an unseen hand has arranged the blooms to look their best. There is a strong fragrance, and a plant in full flower is a wonderful sight.

"Paul's Scarlet"

For nearly forty years this climber from William Paul's Hertfordshire, England nursery was one of the three most popular climbing roses. It was introduced in 1916 from a cross between "Paul's Carmine Pillar" and, possibly, "Rêve d'Or", although it is difficult to see where the scarlet colouring arose from this parentage. A height of 10ft (3m) may be expected on a pillar, while anything up to 20ft (6.1m) is possible on a wall. "Paul's Scarlet" is very adaptable and can be grown successfully in almost any environment, lending itself readily to any form of support.

It is one of the earlier climbers to come into flower, usually shortly after "Gloire de Dijon" opens its first blooms. The mid-green foliage is plentiful but not glossy and a good complement to the semi-double flowers, which are medium sized, up to 2½in (6cm) across, and bright crimson scarlet. The flower colour is held for two or three days, but eventually fades to a somewhat duller shade. The flowers are very profuse, and it is not uncommon for a mature plant to be covered in bloom from top to bottom. Repeat flowering is limited, and it is likely there will be none if it is pruned after flowering; instead, leave well alone until the dormant season. There is a gentle, but not pronounced fragrance. Choose plants only from a top nurseryman as there appears to be loss of vigour with some stocks.

"Purity"

This American-raised rambler was introduced in 1917, and the parentage is recorded as an unnamed seedling pollinated by "Mme. Caroline Testout". "Purity" is nothing like "Mme. Caroline Testout", and it is clear that the unnamed seedling had very close links with

R. wichuraiana. It is, in fact, a typical Wichuraiana, with profuse, close-set, glossy foliage, many thorns and a lateral rather than an upright habit. It is very adaptable and suitable for almost all situations. It is also very hardy and can be grown successfully on a pillar, against a fence, into a tree or even as a free-standing bush to cover an unsightly object. It will make 10ft (3m) on a pillar and 15ft (4.6m) or more climbing into a tree. As its name suggests, the semi-double flowers are of an unblemished, pure white. They are of medium size, rather loose in form but showing attractive yellow stamens when open. The plant is very free flowering for a three-week period, usually beginning at the end of June. As with "Albéric Barbier", a small amount of repeat flowering may be expected late in the season. It has a sweet, refreshing fragrance.

"Sanders White"

"Sanders White" was raised by Sanders and introduced in 1912, and although it has no declared parentage, it is clear from its characteristics that it belongs to the Wichuraiana group of hybrids. It is essentially a lateral grower, with arching stems that will exceed 12ft (3.7m) with support. This rose is very adaptable and hardy, and it can be used in almost all situations. It is even used very effectively as a weeping standard as at the Roseraie de l'Hay in Paris.

The foliage is rather small, but it is deep green, profuse and glossy. The flowers are small, no more than 2in (5cm) across, and the tightly packed petals lie in a neat rosette formation. They are produced in large bunches distributed throughout the plant, which creates a wonderful display for a three-week period. The colour, whiter than white, is brightened by a display of yellow stamens. Although there is no repeat bloom, "Sanders White" adds to its charms with one of the sweetest and strongest perfumes of the whole class of rambling roses.

"Seagull"

Introduced in 1907, "Seagull" has no declared parentage, but there are a great many similarities between it and *R. multiflora,* and it is fairly certain that it is a direct cross between *R. multiflora* and an unknown hybrid. If you like the type of rambler that produces huge heads of bloom but have not enough space for a "Kiftsgate", "Seagull" is the next best thing. Although it will make up to 15ft (4.6m), it will rarely exceed 20ft (6.1m). The foliage is more attractive than that of *R. multiflora,* being larger, fairly glossy and a brighter colour. Flowering lasts for three weeks. The flowers are white, about 1in (25mm) across, and are pleasantly uniform in shape, with ten or twelve rounded petals, which open to reveal a fine display of yellow stamens. The typical sweet *R. multiflora* fragrance is cast into the surrounding air. A good specimen of "Seagull" may be seen growing into a conifer at the Royal National Rose Society headquarters at St Albans, England.

"Souvenir de Claudius Denoyel"

Raised by Frenchman C. Chambard and introduced in 1920, "Souvenir de Claudius Denoyel" is a cross between "Château de Clos Vougeot" and "Commandeur Jules Gravereaux" – a climbing hybrid tea and an old tea rose – and it retains the characteristic red flowers and the cup-shaped blooms of its mother.

The rose will make 12ft (3.7m) if grown on a pillar, but should achieve up to 18ft (5.5m) on a wall. The matt and rather sparse foliage is a little disappointing, but the flowers more than compensate. They are bright crimson, almost appearing to glow, and the heads usually look down on the observer. The flowers have only about twenty petals, so cannot be described as full blooms, but they retain their colour until quite old. The spring bloom is freely borne and thereafter flowers are produced at intervals but never in the quantity to match the first flush. They have a strong, sweet fragrance.

"Veilchenblau"

"Veilchenblau" was raised by J. C. Schmidt of West Germany. Introduced in 1909, it is from a cross between "Crimson Rambler" and "Erinnerung an Brod". "Crimson Rambler" created a sensation when it was first introduced for until then no rambler had had such strong colouring; unfortunately, however, it was prone to mildew, falling from favour after twenty years of popularity. Little is known about "Erinnerung an Brod", but it must have been responsible for the remarkable colouring of "Veilchenblau".

The very green, virtually thornless stems of "Veilchenblau" arch vigorously to climb 15ft (4.6m) into a supporting tree. The foliage is a light, shiny green and has much greater resistance to mildew than "Crimson Rambler". Ideally, grow "Veilchenblau" in partial shade, for its unique colouring does not last when it is exposed to day-long sunshine. The flowers, which generally do not begin to appear until the end of June, are produced in large clusters all over the plant. They are on the small side, a little over 1in (25mm) across, and have many petals, which tend to turn in and lie flat when the flowers are fully open. The colouring changes from a purple-red in the bud to violet-purple in the expanded flower to a slatey-grey at petal fall. When viewed from a distance, the overall effect of the rose is quite blue. Splashes of white frequently appear among the petals, and there is an attractive stamen display. "Veilchenblau" has a sweet, fruity fragrance, which is cast freely into the air.

"William Allen Richardson"

It is believed that an American rose-grower raised a yellow seedling climber from "Rêve d'Or", a straw-yellow, rather tender climber, and sent it to the renowned French nurseryman Veuve Ducher. This seedling sported to produce an orange climber and Ducher named it after the American, William Allen Richardson, and introduced it in 1878.

"William Allen Richardson" is not a strong grower, needing the protection of a sheltered site. However, do not grow it against a warm sunny wall, because it rapidly loses its colour in hot sunshine. It will eventually grow 8–10ft (2.4–3m). The new growth is a rich, dark brown, which turns a pleasant dark green as it matures. The flowers, a full hybrid tea size, both in the number of petals and their length, are an extraordinary deep orange shade particularly towards the flower centre. It was nearly a hundred years before this colour was repeated in a rose. In direct hot sunshine this lovely colouring fades to white. Flowering usually begins after the middle of June, and although there will never be a profusion of blooms, an established plant will go on producing flowers until late autumn.

"Zéphirine Drouhin"

Introduced as long ago as 1868 by the Frenchman, Bizot, it is classified as a bourbon although it has no declared parentage. The bourbons were hybrids of one or two of the China roses and *R. damascena bifera.*

"Zéphirine Drouhin" did not find favour until after World War II, but by 1957 it had risen to the top of England's Rose Society table of repeat-flowering climbers. It may have taken so long to become established because it is not an immediately appealing colour – cerise is often called rosedom's least popular shade. However, it has many good qualities. It is easily controlled, with no thorns to harass the grower, and the growth is steady but restrained so that it can be trained when the time is available. It will ultimately reach 10–12ft (3–3.7m) and will flower until the frosts. The flowering trusses are quite large, with a very good spread of bloom throughout the plant. Although the new foliage is quite bronzy, it is a deep green for much of the season. The semi-double cerise flowers are quite bright, and of medium size, exuding a sweet and powerful fragrance, undoubtedly the rose's most endearing quality. The foliage may well need protection against mildew and blackspot.

MODERN CLIMBING ROSES : 1921 TO THE PRESENT

"Allen Chandler"

A hybrid of "Hugh Dickson" and an unnamed seedling, "Allen Chandler" won a gold medal from England's N.R.S. in 1923, its year of introduction. It has inherited the best qualities of "Hugh Dickson", a somewhat gaunt, hybrid perpetual with beautiful dark red scented flowers, but not the faults. The unnamed seedling has contributed vigour and balance.

A vigorous climber, easily attaining 12ft (3.7m) on a pillar and up to 20ft (6.1m) on a wall, "Allen Chandler" has quite large and plentiful semi-glossy foliage, which will probably need spraying to keep blackspot at bay. Flowering begins early in the season, and there is a heavy first flush of blooms. The flowers, which are quite large, up to 5in (13cm) across, appear in small bunches. The initial form is hybrid tea shaped, but as there are not many petals the deep red, velvety blooms soon open to display lovely golden stamens. It is sad that a rose of this colouring is not strongly scented, but a future breeder may succeed in producing a more fragrant form. It will often have a good crop of bloom in the autumn, and an established plant is rarely out of flower, although it easily runs to seed, which should be quickly removed.

"Aloha"

"Aloha", which was introduced in 1949, was bred by Gene Boerner, the hybridist at Jackson & Perkins, and was the result of a cross between "Mercedes Gallart" and "New Dawn". There is some argument as to whether "Aloha" is a true climber for it takes some time to grow more than 6ft (1.8m), but in time it will. In many ways it is ideal for today's gardens and gardeners, as it is easy to manage and virtually trouble free. On a wall growth of 10ft (3m) may reasonably be expected, but on a pillar growth may not be much over 6ft (1.8m). The excellent foliage is large and glossy and highly resistant to fungal diseases. The large flowers, up to 5in (13cm) across, are initially rather unpromising, for the outer petal is a harsh, unattractive shade of pink and the buds look as though a caterpillar has nibbled off the top. Fortunately, both colour and form improve dramatically as the flower expands. The many petals display a symmetrical form, with the inner petal proving to be a much more attractive shade of pink. As the flower fully opens, a very pretty terracotta centre is revealed. There is a large first flush of flowers around the middle of June and a further good sized crop may be expected in September, with plenty of flowers in between. This is an excellent variety to take indoors as the flowers have a good scent and firm, long stems.

"Altissimo"

It is sad that the rose-buying public rarely chooses plants that have single flowers, and, despite winning a certificate of merit from England's Royal National Rose Society in 1965, "Altissimo" is stocked only by a few nurserymen and it is not very well known.

It was raised by the French firm Delbard-Chabert from a cross between "Tenor" and an unknown rose, and it was introduced in 1966. Like "Aloha", it is suitable for modern gardens, being of restrained, upright growth, reaching about 7ft (2.1m) on a pillar and up to 10ft (3m) on a wall. The dull, medium green foliage is plentiful but may well need spraying to keep blackspot at bay. Flowering commences in spring, continuing almost without respite until late in the season, and although there is never a wealth of bloom, there is a constant, gentle show. The individual blooms repay close study. They are large – up to 5in (13cm) across – very nearly single and a deep, velvety blood red with a bright contrasting display of golden stamens. As the stamens age, they darken and show well against the dark red petals, their beauty being retained to the last.

"Altissimo" would probably enjoy greater popularity if it had a strong fragrance, but such a bright colour is rarely combined with a powerful scent and we must content ourselves with its visual beauty.

"Bantry Bay"

"Bantry Bay" was bred by Sam McGredy and introduced in 1967, when it gained England's Royal National Rose Society certificate of merit. Its parents were "New Dawn", from which it has inherited largely lateral growth, and "Korona", from which it gained an unusual purple blotched stem.

Grown on a wall or fence, it will comfortably attain 12ft (3.7m) laterally and 9–10ft (2.7–3m) vertically. It has plenty of semi-glossy, mid-green foliage, which may need spraying against blackspot, and the semi-double flowers, about 3in (8cm) across, are produced in large trusses. The whole plant should be covered with flowers from top to bottom. The blooms are an attractive shade of light pink with a slightly deeper reverse to the petal. The first flush lasts for several weeks, and thereafter flowers will be produced almost without a break. Although the subsequent flowers are never produced in as great a quantity as the first, quite substantial heads of bloom are produced on vigorous basal shoots until the frosts finally stop them. There is a pleasant, but not strong, wild rose fragrance.

"Casino" ("Gerbe d'Or")

It is fair to say that "Casino" has not quite lived up to its early promise. It is one of only two climbing roses to have gained a gold medal from England's R.N.R.S. since World War II, but it has to be said that, while the rose undoubtedly deserved its award on its performance, it was helped by being grown in the society's sheltered walled garden. Now all climbers in the trials have to cope with the more open and exposed trial ground area. It is significant that "Casino", subsequently planted around the perimeter of this trial area, is struggling to make any impressive growth.

"Casino" was produced from "Coral Dawn", itself a climber, and "Buccaneer", a tall yellow hybrid tea from the United States. It has inherited its colouring largely from "Buccaneer" and its climbing qualities from both parents. Protected by a wall, it will climb to 12ft (3.7m), but it is not recommended as a pillar rose in an exposed situation. Its distinctive glossy, light green foliage will need spraying in districts affected by blackspot. The first flush of blooms will appear early in the season, and there will nearly always be some flowers appearing thereafter, although never with quite the same freedom as at first. The large, full-petalled flowers have an unusual, almost old-fashioned shape, and they are a soft but very rich and pure yellow. Its refreshing but soapy fragrance is not liked by everyone.

"Compassion"

"Compassion" was bred by Jack Harkness at his Hertfordshire nursery, and it won a R.N.R.S. trial ground certificate in 1972 and the Henry Edland medal for the most fragrant rose on trial in 1973. Harkness could hardly have expected such a rose to result from the parent plants he selected: "White Cockade", a semi-climber, and "Prima Ballerina", a pink, large flowered rose. "Compassion" has more vigour than "White Cockade" and is a more attractive pink than "Prima Ballerina"; it has also apparently inherited extra vigour from "New Dawn", one of the parents of "White Cockade".

"Compassion" must be very close to being

the best climber bred since World War II. It will constantly produce new basal growth, thus escaping the rather barren appearance of many climbers. It will steadily, but not rampantly, make its way upwards, achieving 10ft (3m) as a pillar and up to 15ft (4.6m) on a wall. The foliage, an attractive glossy, dark green is produced in abundance from top to bottom. Harkness once described it as "so clean that you could eat your dinner off it!" It may not always reach that standard, but it is fair to say that it is much more disease resistant than most. The flowers are produced from the beginning of June, and it has two large flushes in June and September with many flowers between and after these months. The large flowers, often classically formed, have nearly forty petals. The early flowers are a fairly ordinary shade of pink, but from August the blooms are a much richer shade of salmon-apricot, and the plant positively glows with these later flowers. The fragrance, which is heavy and satisfying close to, is not freely cast into the air.

"Copenhagen"

"Copenhagen" won a certificate of merit from England's Royal National Rose Society in 1963 and many nurserymen immediately added this bright red, fragrant and repeat-flowering climber to their catalogues. But by 1980 it had been dropped from the Royal National Rose Society's list of popular climbing and rambling roses, largely because it is a little temperamental, thriving only when it is happy with its situation, takes several years to get established and may take five or six to grow more than 6ft (1.8m).

It was the first major success of Danish rose grower Niels Poulsen, and it arose from a cross between an unknown seedling (presumably with climbing blood in it) and "Ena Harkness", which has passed on its colouring, fragrance and foliage characteristics. In the right situation it will ultimately reach 10ft (3m) on a wall and perhaps 7ft (2.1m) on a pillar.

Although there is never a wealth of bloom, flowers are produced in groups during the entire season. The wonderfully bright, deep scarlet flowers are rather special: they are large, with up to fifty petals, but shapely, and the coppery foliage, which is not profuse, blends perfectly with the blooms. As well as its rich fragrance, "Copenhagen" has its good health to recommend it.

"Crimson Glory"

The bush rose "Crimson Glory" was regarded as a milestone in the breeding of roses when it was introduced in 1935. It was the first deep crimson, velvety bush of real quality and represented a considerable advance on all its predecessors. Bred from a "Catherine Kordes" seedling with pollen provided by "W. E. Chaplin", another deep crimson rose, it became recognized as the outstandingly fragrant rose for more than a decade and was used by nearly all the world's rose breeders.

The climbing sport was introduced by Jackson & Perkins in 1946. On a wall it will achieve a height of 10ft (3m), but avoid a south wall as strong sunlight makes the flower colour less appealing. Blooms are produced early in the season more or less continuously until the first sharp frosts. There is never a profusion of bloom, but on the majority of flowering days it is possible to select a wonderful buttonhole rose. The medium to large blooms have a fine form, and the lovely deep velvety crimson colour combines with the overwhelming fragrance to provide an unforgettable rose.

"Crimson Shower"

This climber or, more accurately, rambler, was almost the last of a line of very pliant-stemmed roses that began to appear at the turn of the century. It was bred by English rosarian Albert Norman, who wrote of the difficulties of producing roses like "Crimson Shower", which, to be evaluated properly, had to be grown for a number of years and which grew ever larger, taking up more and more garden space. We can be thankful that he persevered, for "Crimson Shower" is the best of this type of rose.

It was bred from a cross with "Excelsa", another pliant-stemmed rambler and was introduced in 1951. It will grow strongly in nearly all situations, comfortably reaching 15ft (4.6m) if supported by a wall. Thanks to its pliant stems, it is very adaptable and looks particularly effective as a weeping standard. The small, profuse and glossy foliage is much less prone to mildew than most roses of this type. "Crimson Shower" does not begin to flower until late, but it then goes on until late autumn. The small flowers, not much over 1in (25mm) across, have plenty of petals and are produced in substantial clusters. The rich crimson colour provides an impressive spectacle when the plant is at peak flowering, but unfortunately there is not much scent.

"Danse des Sylphes"

After his success with "Danse du Feu", it was logical that Charles Mallerin should attempt to do it again, and in 1957 he produced "Danse des Sylphes", which won awards at both the Paris-Bagatelle and Madrid rose trials. It has, however, been slow to gain recognition in the United Kingdom.

Bred from "Danse du Feu" crossed with a seedling from "Peace" and "Independence", "Danse des Sylphes" is almost as vigorous as "Danse du Feu" and will eventually reach 10ft (3m) on a wall. Its plentiful, semi-glossy foliage clothes the plant from top to bottom, and there is no ugly barren patch at the base. Flowering usually begins early and is soon at its peak. The medium sized flowers are usually produced in threes and fours, and the flowers themselves are noticeably rounded with symmetrically arranged petals. The colour, somewhere between crimson and scarlet, fades much less objectionably than does that of "Danse du Feu". During its first flowering period the whole plant should be covered in bloom from top to bottom, but thereafter flowering is never again as profuse, although satisfactory flushes are produced until late in the season.

"Danse du Feu" ("Spectacular")

Raised by Frenchman Charles Mallerin,

"Danse du Feu" was introduced in 1953. Almost immediately it won recognition in several countries, and it is still well regarded in most of Europe and the United States.

The declared parentage is "Paul's Scarlet Climber" with a *R. multiflora* seedling; the latter must have contributed valuable genes to help produce a repeat-flowering climber.

"Danse du Feu", a vigorous but not rampant climber, will grow in nearly all situations and should reach 10ft (3m) on a wall. Flowering begins early, and quite soon the plant is a spectacular mass of flower.

The semi-double, medium sized flowers are initially a splendid bright orange-scarlet, but after a few days, less in hot sun, the colour is less than spectacular – the rose's detractors call it an objectionable muddy red.

In addition, "Danse du Feu" is reluctant to release its petals and in wet weather can look a sorry sight. After the first large flush of flowers, clusters of blooms will continue to appear, although never again in the original volume. The plentiful, semi-glossy and medium green foliage is very healthy.

"Don Juan"

Highly regarded in the United States, where it has had a rating of 8.1, and in Europe, "Don Juan" is not very well known in the United Kingdom. It resulted from a cross between a "New Dawn" seedling and "New Yorker", which contributed colour, fragrance and large flowers, while "New Dawn" passed on its climbing habit.

"Don Juan" is of medium vigour, eventually reaching 8ft (2.4m) as a pillar rose and over 10ft (3m) on a wall. The semi-glossy foliage is moderately abundant but somewhat leathery. The flowers, which can be up to 5in (13cm) across, are usually produced in small clusters, and they are of a lovely velvety crimson with a good strong perfume. Although repeat flowering is satisfactory, the second crop does not equal the first, and the flowers are not happy in the wet, a fact that has undoubtedly contributed towards its lack of recognition in the United Kingdom.

"Dortmund"

It is extraordinary that twice as many U.K. nurserymen sell "American Pillar", a once-flowering rambler, as stock and sell this similar but repeat-flowering climber. "Dortmund" is the result of a cross between a seedling and *R. kordesii,* and the Kordesii climbers were bred primarily to combat the harsh winters experienced in north Europe.

"Dortmund" grows to medium height: about 10ft (3m) on a wall, 7–8ft (2.4m) on a pillar or 6ft (1.8m) as a hedge. Spring brings a splendid display for several weeks. After the first flush, it is essential that the developing hips are removed because "Dortmund" very readily sets seed, and if these are allowed to develop, they will inhibit future flowering. Additional flushes can be expected when dead-headed. The single, blood red flowers, which are up to 4in (10cm) across, have a pronounced white eye at the base of the petals, against which the yellow stamens are very attractively displayed. The foliage is wonderful, being dense, glossy and deep green, almost holly-like in appearance. Like other Kordesii climbers, "Dortmund" is exceptionally resistant to blackspot and mildew.

"Dream Girl"

This rose is raised from a cross between "Dr W. van Fleet" and "Señora Gari". It is a climber of average height, rarely exceeding 10ft (3m) and since it takes several years to achieve that, it is well suited to areas where only moderate growth is required. The flowers are medium sized, 3–4in (8–10cm) across, mostly produced in small trusses. The plentiful petals are an attractive salmon-pink with yellow tints, and they have a very pleasant scent. Although there is rarely an abundance of bloom, "Dream Girl" will go on producing flowers over a long period. The large and glossy foliage is reputed to be disease resistant.

"Dreaming Spires"

"Dreaming Spires" originated at the nursery of the Mattock brothers near Oxford, England. It was introduced in 1973 and subsequently won an award at the Belfast International Rose Trials. It has not, however, gained a great following, possibly because, although the plant flowers continuously throughout the summer and autumn, there is rarely a spectacular wealth of bloom.

Growth is above average, and 10ft (3m) on a pillar or 12ft (3.7m) on a wall may be expected. In flower early in milder climates, it will go on producing blooms until the frosts call a halt. The full flowers, up to 5in (13cm) across, are a deep yellow with a pale orange flush to the petal edges, but in hot sun the colour is not very stable and an east or west wall is to be preferred. "Dreaming Spires" has a noticeable fragrance and attractive deep green, glossy foliage.

"Dublin Bay"

A cross between "Bantry Bay" and "Altissimo", "Dublin Bay" was bred by Sam McGredy and introduced in 1976, having won a R.N.R.S. trial ground certificate in 1974. It will not make a very large plant and indeed has been criticized in some quarters for behaving more like a shrub than a climber. Be patient, because you may well have to wait several years for it to reach a height of 7ft (2.1m) or more.

Usually in flower before the main flush of climbers, it will produce a profusion of bloom at its first flowering, with a second large crop and several blooms before and after. The bright, deep red flowers have up to twenty-five petals in an attractive form 4in (10cm) across. There is a slightly tangy, but not particularly memorable, scent. "Dublin Bay" has a good display of dark green, glossy foliage, which covers the plant almost to its base, and it has the added advantage of being very disease resistant.

"Ena Harkness"

The climber is a sport of the original bush, which, when introduced in 1946, was the outstanding large flowered red bush rose for nearly twenty years. "Ena Harkness" had both colour and fragrance, but one flaw that was unacceptable in a bush rose – the stems supporting the blooms were not firm, and the rose often flopped untidily. But this weakness in a bush is a most decided asset in a climber, as the majority of the blooms will be above the head of the viewer.

Climbing sports of "Ena Harkness" have appeared in more than one nursery, but most of those now distributed came from the nursery of R. Murrell from Hemel Hempstead, Hertfordshire, England. Climbing "Ena Harkness", which was introduced in 1954, often has larger blooms than the bush form – they can exceed 6in (15cm) across. It will comfortably achieve 10ft (3m) on a wall and flowers in early June. There is a large first flush and quite a satisfactory repeat in early autumn, with occasional blooms between the main flushes. The flowers are a very distinctive deep, rich, bright crimson scarlet and have a strong and satisfying damask-type fragrance. The blooms cope with extremes of weather very well, opening in the wet and fading but little in hot sunshine. The least satisfactory aspect of this rose is the foliage, which is mid-green, rather limp and likely to get blackspot.

"Fugue"

Although it won a gold medal in the Madrid trials in 1958, "Fugue" is much more popular in Europe than in the United Kingdom or the U.S.A., and at present no U.K. nurseryman appears to stock it. It was bred by the Meilland nursery and is the result of a cross between "Alain" and "Guinée". "Alain" is a bright red cluster-flowered rose, which was popular all over Europe for several years.

More upright than lateral, "Fugue" will achieve a height slightly over 10ft (3m). The oval, semi-glossy and fairly dark foliage is plentiful. In the south of England "Fugue" flowers early, and a very good display will follow. The semi-double flowers are not much more than 3in (8cm) across and open wide and flat. The bright scarlet crimson blooms have some scent but are not markedly fragrant. The repeat flower is better than that of "Guinée", but the second flowering does not equal the first.

"Galway Bay"

Introduced in 1966, "Galway Bay" is one of a number of climbers that Sam McGredy bred from "Heidelberg", a tall, bright crimson shrub. The other parent was "Queen Elizabeth", a tall-growing rose.

"Galway Bay" is an ideal pillar rose or a climber to grow in a narrow space, for nearly all its growth is vertical and there is little lateral growth. Basal shoots are freely produced, and there is never a problem with the base of the tree becoming bare. The large, plentiful, mid-green foliage is evenly borne and will amply cover the plant. It should be in full flower early. The largest trusses are produced on the basal shoots, although flowering is spread throughout the plant, which should eventually reach about 10ft (3m). The medium sized flowers, which are fairly full, pleasantly formed and slightly globular, are predominantly reddish-pink with a deeper reverse to the petal. After the first flush, large basal trusses of bloom are produced until well into autumn, and the plant is out of flower only for short intervals. There is a pleasant but not remarkable fragrance.

Remember, however, that like so many of the offspring of "Heidelberg", "Galway Bay" is prone to blackspot, so you must be prepared to spray it.

"Golden Showers"

This is one of the most popular and universally admired of all climbing roses. Certainly in the United Kingdom it is the most popular yellow climber. It was introduced in 1956 and bred from "Charlotte Armstrong", a red hybrid tea, and "Captain Thomas", a U.S. yellow climber. The two created a rose that is ideal for today's gardens: it is very free flowering, a good colour and easily managed.

Had it been raised in the United Kingdom, "Golden Showers" would most probably have been classified as a shrub. Grown against a pillar, it will take several years to exceed 6ft (1.8m), but on a wall it will exceed 12ft (3.7m). It is predominantly an upright grower, but with care it can be encouraged to fill a lateral space. Its critics would say that its foliage is rather thin, but the light green colour is attractive and fairly disease resistant although it is not immune to fungal diseases. The plant has two main flushes, when flowers are borne in profusion, but in the flowering season it is hardly ever without blooms and is one of the very best for carrying flowers low down. The bright lemon-yellow flowers are quite large, up to 4in (10cm) across, but they open very quickly as there are not many petals. In hot sun the colour fades rather too quickly and the flowers can finish nearly white. It has a sweet, but not strong, lemon fragrance, and there is a pretty stamen display from the red anthers.

"Guinée"

Introduced in 1938, "Guinée" is a cross between "Souvenir de Claudius Denoyel" and "Ami Quinard", a dark crimson hybrid tea.

"Guinée" is a strong grower, capable of reaching 20ft (6.1m) in a situation it likes. However, choose its position with care because against a dark background the flowers will be scarcely visible. The foliage is mid-green, semi-glossy and thick textured, but it may get mildew so spraying is necessary. It is fairly early into bloom and will have quite a large, evenly spaced crop for several weeks. There-after random blooms are produced into late autumn, but you will be lucky if more than a few appear at a time. The flowers are the darkest red imaginable with a velvet sheen to the petals. They are quite large, up to 4½in (11cm) across, with plenty of petals and an attractive form, which finishes flat with a display of yellow stamens. The flowers remain outstanding even in the hottest sun, showing none of the scorch or "blueing" that is common in roses of this colour. To add to the joy of

the blooms there is a deep and penetrating fragrance of the type usually associated with red roses.

"Handel"

This must be almost the most popular, if not *the* most popular of all climbing roses. It has a very high rating in the United States, is sold all over Europe and is a long way ahead in England's Royal National Rose Society table of popular perpetual climbing roses. "Handel" is a cross between the shrub rose "Heidelberg" and the floribunda "Columbine", to which much of the delightful and original colouring seen in "Handel" can be attributed. "Columbine" is creamy-yellow with a pink edge to the petal, and it is this pink edging that has made "Handel" such a delightful climbing rose.

"Handel" was introduced in 1965 and in the same year won a trial ground certificate from England's R.N.R.S. It is very reliable and will climb in almost all circumstances, making up to 20ft (6.1m) in most areas of the United States, although 10–12ft (3–3.7m) is more likely in the United Kingdom. The dark green, glossy foliage is quite profuse and leathery, but like nearly all roses bred from "Heidelberg" it needs to be sprayed to keep blackspot at bay. The first flowers appear in mid-season, when there is a good, even display. There is an almost equally good crop in September, and many flowers can be expected before and after the autumn flowering. The medium sized flowers open from shapely buds to about twenty predominantly cream petals with a delightful pink edge. If only this delightful colouring remained until petal fall, but sadly, and especially in hot sunshine, this pink edging rapidly bleaches and the flowers lose their charm. There is not much scent, but the flowers do have the ability to withstand rainfall.

"Iceberg"

This is one of the most satisfactory of climbing sports. "Iceberg" the bush was an epoch-making rose, a cross between the old hybrid musk shrub rose "Robin Hood" and the white, classically shaped hybrid tea "Virgo". "Robin Hood" bears a profusion of flowers in very large trusses and has transmitted the profuse flowering to "Iceberg", but while all the hybrid musks flower profusely and then have a long rest, "Iceberg" produces new flowers at regular intervals.

The climbing sport was introduced in 1968 and was awarded a trial ground certificate in 1969. Climbing "Iceberg" will achieve 12ft (3.7m) on a wall and is probably best grown with this support as there are reports of shy flowering when it is grown against a pillar. There is a heavy first flush, but quantities of repeat flowers do seem to depend on the age of the plant, and it may take several years before repeat flowering of any quantity is achieved. The white flowers are sometimes flushed with pink and have a light scent. The attractive light green foliage will need spraying to keep blackspot and mildew at bay.

"Iskra" ("Sparkling Scarlet")

Although it is not well known in the United Kingdom, "Sparkling Scarlet" is one of the most popular roses in parts of Europe, where it has won several awards: a certificate from Geneva, a first certificate from Lyons and the top award and a gold medal from the Paris-Bagatelle trials, all in 1969. It was raised by the Meilland nursery and introduced in 1970, the result of a cross between "Danse des Sylphes" and "Zambra", an orange cluster-flowered rose.

"Sparkling Scarlet" is another of those climbers of only medium vigour, and it will take a number of years to exceed 8ft (2.4m). The plentiful, mid-green foliage, which is initially quite bronzy, has a slight tendency to mildew, but this is easily cured. The first flowers appear quite early in the season, and an established plant will provide a profuse display. The flowers, which have ten to fifteen petals, are on the small side, but the brilliant colour, a sparkling scarlet, has tremendous impact. It is impossible to say yet if a large plant will produce a good crop of repeat flowers, but all the indications are that the second flush will rival the first.

"John Cabot"

Awarded a certificate of merit in England's 1985 R.N.R.S. trials, this rose is completely new to the U.K. and not commercially available as in Canada and the U.S.A.

It was introduced as long ago as 1978 in Canada and raised at the Canadian Department of Agriculture, Ottawa, which specializes in breeding roses able to withstand the Canadian winter. The two plants on trial at St Albans suggest that "John Cabot" will spread laterally as much as vertically. Growth of 8ft (2.4m) has been achieved, but it seems likely that more would be possible on a wall. The plentiful foliage is a pleasant light green, and it appears to be disease resistant. Flowers are on the small side, about $2\frac{1}{2}$in (6cm) across, but they are produced in profusion all over the plant. Each bloom has about forty petals, and they open fairly flat. The mauvy-red colour might more accurately be described as magenta, which is a new colour for repeat-flowering climbers, and there is a good fragrance. First reports indicate that the repeat flowering is good.

"Joseph's Coat"

Although "Joseph's Coat" is classified as a semi-climber in the United Kingdom, given the support of a wall, it will climb quite satisfactorily. Against a wall, "Joseph's Coat" will spread laterally 6ft (1.8m) in both directions and to about the same height, and this is one of the most satisfactory ways to grow this rose, giving a wide spread of colour. Vertically it will reach 10ft (3m) but not exceed it. It can be equally effectively grown as a free-standing shrub, when it will achieve a spread of 5ft (1.5m) and as much, if not more, vertically.

"Joseph's Coat" was produced from the seed of "Buccaneer" and the pollen of "Circus", which contributed much to its rare and startling colour.

The mid-green, semi-glossy foliage, which is quite large and somewhat rounded in shape, covers the plant very satisfactorily. There are two large crops of bloom, although usually quite a gap between crops, with the flowers beginning a bright yellow with orange flushes, changing to a rich orange-red and finishing a reddish-pink. This is a much more satisfying colour cavalcade than that of most of the multi-hued roses. At no stage does the colouring become dull and muddy, a common fault of this type of flower. It has a light but tangy and pleasant fragrance.

"Kordista"

Unnamed and as yet unproven, "Kordista" won an English Royal National Rose Society trial ground certificate in 1985 but it is unlikely to be introduced before 1988. However, I believe it is a climber that will soon become popular.

"Kordista" has a complex parentage that includes two or three batches of climbing genes. Two seedling crosses – "Little Darling" × "Goldilocks" and "Eva" × "Reveil Dijonnais" – were finally pollinated by "Gold-stern", the yellow Kordesii climber.

At St Albans "Kordista" achieved a height a little in excess of 8ft (2.4m) and had a very good covering of mid-green foliage. A spread of bloom throughout the plant at the first flowering was followed by a smaller second flush. The semi-double flowers, about 3in (8cm) across, are a most attractive orange-pink, but the rose tends to hang on to its petals too long, slightly spoiling the overall effect.

"Lady Barbara"

Not yet commercially available, "Lady Barbara" gained a certificate of merit at the Geneva trials in 1984 and the international jury awarded it 51.9 points out of a possible maximum of 60.

This may be a rose that will grow better in a warmer climate than the United Kingdom enjoys, and nurserymen in several countries are growing it on trial. It has an involved parentage. "Red Planet", the dark red, large flowered rose, was pollinated by a semi-climber seedling, which arose from "Elizabeth of Glamis" pollinated by a "Galway Bay" × "Sutters Gold".

"Lady Barbara" is an upright grower, and at Geneva in its three years of trial it reached 10ft (3m) on a metal pillar. It should reach 10ft (3m) on a wall in the United Kingdom. In early July in Geneva it had flowers from top to bottom, and in the middle of August it was showing plenty of new bloom. The hybrid tea shaped blooms, which are usually about 4in (10cm) across, are produced in medium sized trusses, and the colour is completely new for a climbing rose – tangerine-orange with a yellow reverse. The foliage is glossy, but is not entirely satisfactory, as ideally, it should be more profuse. There is a significant fruity fragrance.

"Lavinia" ("Tanklewi")

Introduced to the United Kingdom rose market as recently as 1983, this climber, like other roses from the Tantau nursery, does not have a declared parentage. The practice of failing to declare the parentage of new seedlings is disappointing for both rose growers and rose breeders, and it does make the whole process of rose breeding less scientific.

The overall impression made by "Lavinia" is of semi-glossiness with close-set leaves and a good covering of foliage over the whole plant. The distinctive light green foliage darkens with age. It is a slightly more upright than lateral grower and should reach 10ft (3m) on a wall. The blooms are a little larger than those usually found on pink climbers, and they have a pretty rounded form and around twenty petals. "Lavinia" is distinguished from the other pink climbers introduced in the last twenty years by its freedom of flowering and its delightful shade of pink. The repeat-flowering characteristics are not yet fully tested, but early indications are promising. It may get a little blackspot and mildew, but its disease resistance is generally above average. There is a light, but not pronounced, wild rose fragrance.

"Leverkusen"

One of the very earliest Kordesii varieties to be introduced (in 1954), "Leverkusen" arose from a cross between R. kordesii and "Golden Glow".

A climber of medium height, "Leverkusen" usually reaches 10ft (3m) but rarely exceeds 12ft (3.7m). It is very tough and hardy and can be grown in virtually any position and against any type of support, even growing effectively as a free-standing shrub. The shiny, light green foliage has excellent disease resistance, and only in badly affected areas should it need spraying for blackspot. Although the foliage is on the small side, it clothes the plant almost from top to bottom. It comes into flower a little later than most, but the freedom of bloom from this first flowering is very impressive, with an even spread over the whole plant. The lemon-yellow flowers, which have a deeper cast at the centre, appear in small, graceful trusses. The flowers are medium sized with over twenty petals, and they cope very successfully with extremes of weather. After the first flowering there can be a long wait, but mature plants should eventually produce a repeat, although this is often disappointing. The lemon-coloured flowers are complemented by a lemon fragrance.

"Mme. Grégoire Staechelin"

One of only three once-flowering roses included in this group of climbing roses, "Mme. Grégoire Staechelin" was bred by the famous Spanish breeder, Pedro Dot, and introduced in 1927. It is known also as "Spanish Beauty" but is more often known by its original name in English-speaking countries. It resulted from a cross between "Frau Karl Druschki" and "Château de Clos Vougeot".

"Mme. Grégoire Staechelin" is a very strong grower, achieving up to 20ft (6.1m) on a wall, and it is one of the few climbing roses that will flourish on a north wall. The large and plentiful, semi-glossy foliage is a pleasing mid-green and healthier than most. It is early into flower, the large flowers being of quite exceptional beauty. Dark pink buds open to reveal slightly ruffled flowers, with glowing light pink inner petals assuming light yellow hues towards the base. The combination of light pink and yellow petals and the stamen display is one of the glories of the rose season. A large plant will have bunches of flowers all along its branches, which because of the weight and size of the blooms, tend to hang slightly downwards to give the ground onlooker an even better view. There is a delightful sweet fragrance as an added bonus.

"Mme. Grégoire Staechelin" has to be managed carefully to ensure that a large expanse of bare stem does not develop. It cannot be recommended for a pillar, but is best grown on a wall where the new growth can be pulled sideways and tied in a near-horizontal position. Eventually one or two of the main stems may have to be cut right down to encourage more basal activity. There are no repeat flowers, but an enormous display of hips is produced, which eventually turn light orange.

"Maigold"

How many delights has this rose? It is in bloom before nearly all others, it has lovely colouring, intoxicating fragrance and radiant shiny foliage, and it has a robust character.

The parentage of this rose is the floribunda "Poulsen's Pink" pollinated by the summer-flowering shrub "Frühlingstag", the latter bred from "McGredy's Wonder" pollinated by "Frühlingsgold", which have undoubtedly contributed towards the strong and attractive colouring shown by "Maigold". "Maigold" was introduced in 1953, and it won an award from the R.N.R.S. in the same year.

It is often described as being shrubby, but against a wall it will reach 15ft (4.6m). It can grow equally successfully against a wall or a pillar, or as a shrub. The shiny green foliage is a great attraction; it is very thick in texture, with tooth-like incisions, and is borne profusely throughout the plant. It is, however, very thorny, and should be tackled only if you are wearing a good pair of gloves. You will be unlucky if it is not in flower early in the season, and for the next five or six weeks there will be a wonderful display. There are red streaks in the bud, but blooms fairly quickly open into a glorious bronzy-yellow with a fine display of stamens. The medium sized blooms have a most unusual fragrance, somewhat resembling soapy honey. "Maigold" is often described as having very little repeat, but it may be possible to encourage a good repeat show by dead-heading as quickly as possible before any plant energy goes into the formation of seed pods.

"Meg"

Introduced in 1955, "Meg" won England's National Rose Society's trial ground certificate in 1954 and a gold medal in the same year. It has large, sumptuous blooms and delightful colouring, but the repeat-flowering qualities can often be disappointing, and while we can exult in this climber's beauty we must enjoy the blooms when we can. There is some doubt about the parentage, but it is believed to be "Paul's Lemon Pillar" pollinated by "Madame Butterfly", a beautiful pale pink, large flowered rose. "Meg" will reach 12ft (3.7m) on a wall, but it is not easy to train because of its rigid stems and is best grown against a wall or informally into a tree. The foliage is more matt than glossy, and is not therefore particularly striking, but it gives good overall coverage.

Flowering is mid-season, and, like "Mermaid", "Meg" will never bloom in large quantities. The beauty of the individual blooms is almost unsurpassed, however. About ten petals open wide to present a large boss of stamens, which darken dramatically towards their base. The flower colour is a delightful salmon-apricot with a yellow sunset effect as the petals approach the stamens. There is a noticeable fragrance. Dead-heading must be done immediately if there is to be any repeat bloom.

"Morgengruss"

Introduced in 1962, "Morgengruss" is largely unknown in the United Kingdom but became popular and successful in the United States, where it was given the very high rating of 9.0. It is another Kordesii rose, resulting from *R. kordesii* pollinated by "Cleopatra", a vivid, bi-colour large flowered rose, bright in colour but rather thin in growth, which does not appear to have had much direct influence on the characteristics of "Morgengruss".

A row of maiden plants of "Morgengruss" would make you think that it was no more than a rather sprawly shrub, for in its first year or two it does not make a great deal of growth. Thereafter it will send out long lateral shoots, which can be trained upwards to exceed 10ft (3m) or sideways to cover a substantial wall space.

"Morgengruss" has delightful, light green, shiny and very healthy foliage, a shade of green that I cannot recall seeing in any other rose. The full-petalled flowers start to appear a little after the earliest to bloom, fawn buds opening to a confection of pinks and buffs. The flowers are pleasingly irregular in form, quite large, 4in (10cm) across, and have an unusual, but to some tastes not particularly appealing, fragrance. There will be a profusion of bloom at the first flowering and a very satisfactory repeat in the autumn. "Morgengruss" must be one of, if not the very best, of the Kordesii climbers.

"Morning Jewel"

"Morning Jewel" has never been a great commercial success; there were probably too many pink climbing roses already available when it was introduced in 1968, but several British nurserymen stock it. It arose from a cross between "New Dawn" and "Red Dandy".

Predominantly a lateral grower, it is a very suitable choice for covering a fence, but it will eventually reach 10ft (3m) on a wall. Its excellent glossy foliage gives the plant a very good covering. Usually in flower before the longest day and with a profuse first flowering, the whole plant is a picture of colour. The semi-double flowers are up to 4in (10cm) across and are a bright glowing pink. The bud form is good, and the flowers have pleasantly rounded petals which, when fully expanded, give an attractive stamen display. The colour holds satisfactorily, and there is a noticeable but not particularly significant fragrance. Although there are many later flowers, the profusion of the early flowering is never repeated. As "Morning Jewel" produces plenty of basal growth, there is never a problem with a barren area at the bottom of the plant.

126

"Mrs Sam McGredy"

The bush form "Mrs Sam McGredy" has an involved parentage: "Donald McDonald" was pollinated by "Golden Emblem"; the resulting seedling was pollinated by another seedling, which arose from an unknown seedling pollinated by "The Queen Alexandra Rose". The unique colouring of "Mrs Sam McGredy" was largely attributed to "The Queen Alexandra Rose".

The bush rose sported first into a climber in Holland, with a second sport occurring in the United States. The Dutch sport was introduced in 1937; the American in 1940.

Climbing "Mrs Sam McGredy" will usually reach 10ft (3m), and it can achieve growth up to 15ft (4.6m) on a favourable wall. The attractive, deep plum-red foliage, which is particularly evident when young, sadly needs spraying regularly to keep blackspot at bay. It has a profuse first flowering, and the large salmon-scarlet flowers make a glorious spectacle. This rare colouring has not to this day been recaptured in any modern rose. It has a pleasant but not strong fragrance. Although there is usually quite a gap before any repeat flower, you will be unlucky if there are no later blooms.

"New Dawn"

Aptly named, "New Dawn" may be considered the beginning of a new era in the development of perpetual climbing roses, for of those introduced since it first appeared nearly half claim "New Dawn" in their ancestry. It arose as a perpetual sport of the vigorous but once-flowering climbing rose, "Dr W. van Fleet" and was introduced in 1930. "Dr W. van Fleet" was bred from *R. wichuraiana*, pollinated by the old tea rose "Safrano", and this seedling in its turn was pollinated by the pink hybrid tea "Souvenir du Président Carnot". Theoretically, "Dr W. van Fleet" and "New Dawn" ought to be infertile, but in fact both are exceptionally fertile.

"New Dawn" has remained popular for over fifty years, a tribute to its freedom of flower, sweet scent, charm and excellent health. It is very adaptable, equally happy on a pillar, on a wall or sprawling all over a fence. It is predominantly a lateral grower, but it can exceed a height of 20ft (6.1m) on a house wall. Its shiny, light green foliage is very disease resistant. The plant is hardy, thriving in positions where others will give up the struggle. The flowers begin to appear a little later than most, but there is usually a profuse spring display. The medium sized blooms are a pretty apple-blossom pink with a deeper pink centre, and they have a sweet and refreshing fragrance, reminiscent of fruit blossom. After the first flush, there is a continuous production of blooms, with basal shoots always producing flowering trusses. The heavy first crop is never equalled, but the plant is scarcely ever without some flowers.

"Nozomi"

Although it is a once-flowering rose, "Nozomi" is in flower for a long period. Moreover, it has many excellent qualities and is too good a rose to overlook. "Nozomi", which is Japanese for "hope", was bred from "Fairy Princess", a climbing miniature that rarely exceeds 3ft (0.9m), and "Sweet Fairy", which, as the name suggests, is a fragrant miniature. The rare and fascinating ground-hugging characteristic of *R. wichuraiana*, which is in the ancestry of "Fairy Princess", has been handed on to "Nozomi", which was introduced in 1968.

"Nozomi" is fairly early into flower and the plant is soon smothered with bloom. The flowering period goes on for about six weeks and then, more often than not, there will be no more bloom. Occasionally, however, well established plants will give a few more flowers late in the season. It will sometimes repeat when grown as a weeping standard. Against a house wall it will grow over 6ft (1.8m) in height and an equal distance along the ground. The rather dainty, pointed foliage is glossy and miniature, but it is prone to blackspot and will, more often than not, pass on this characteristic to roses bred from it. The tiny flowers are single and a delicate shade of pink.

"Parade"

This American rose appeared in 1953 and was introduced to the United Kingdom in 1955. It has, however, never become very popular in the United Kingdom, possibly because of its colour, but it is a first-class garden plant and one of the most reliable and trouble free climbers available. It is more popular in the United States, where it has been given a rating of 7.9. It arose from a cross between a "New Dawn" seedling and climbing "World's Fair", a Kordes-raised, cluster-flowered, very dark red rose.

"Parade" is hardy and adaptable, and as it is said even to cope well with shade, it is a good choice for a north wall. In favourable conditions it will achieve 12ft (3.7m). The plentiful, semi-glossy, dark green foliage has a strong reddish tint when it is new.

It should be in full flower in the spring, and a large spread of bloom will be produced. There is a second large crop in autumn and frequently flowers between the main flushes. The flowers are full, nicely rounded when open and quite large, up to 4in (10cm) across, but they are a carmine or deep pink, which is not a favourite colour among rose growers. The weight of the flower will often cause the stem to nod, a most desirable characteristic for a climbing rose. The fragrance is quite strong, but it is not everyone's favourite.

"Parkdirektor Riggers"

This outstandingly colourful and vigorous rose took several years to become accepted in the United Kingdom, but it is now popular in nearly all rose-growing countries. Raised by Wilhelm Kordes and introduced in 1957, it is a cross between R. kordesii and "Our Princess", a crimson cluster-flowered rose, which has passed on its bright red colour and free blooming characteristic. "Parkdirektor Riggers" is one of the most vigorous of the repeat-flowering climbers, reaching 15ft (4.6m) on a wall; growth of 20ft (6.1m) is probably not beyond it.

The foliage is a very deep green, almost black, and it is, to all appearances, shiny and healthy. Alas however, "Parkdirektor Riggers" will succumb to both blackspot and mildew in unfavourable circumstances, although it continues to grow through any attack. The flowers, which are borne in medium sized clusters, first appear a little later than most, and they eventually spread throughout the plant to produce a spectacular display. The flowers, which are up to 3in (8cm) across, have about fifteen petals and are a vivid, unfading scarlet crimson. At the centre yellow stamens contrast with a white blotch at the base of the petals. Blooms are occasionally produced during the second half of summer, but "Parkdirektor Riggers" really excels again in early autumn, when the flush of bloom will often equal the first. There is a slight Kordesii-type scent.

"Phyllis Bide"

Introduced in 1923, "Phyllis Bide" is reputed to be a cross between "Perle d'Or" and "Gloire de Dijon". "Perle d'Or" is a pretty apricot old China rose with R. multiflora in its ancestry, and the climbing ability of "Phyllis Bide" is almost certainly inherited from R. multiflora.

"Phyllis Bide" does not usually grow very tall, 8ft (2.4m) being more likely than 10ft (3m), although Graham Thomas suggested that it could grow to 12ft (3.7m). The plant has a dainty airiness, the small but reasonably profuse foliage matched by sprays of little flowers not much larger than those of a miniature rose. Although it is predominantly pastel in the depth of colour, the combination of yellow-pink and pale gold is very pretty. "Phyllis Bide" is never profusely in bloom, but the flowers are produced at intermittent intervals until quite late in the season. There is a light but sweet scent.

"Pink Perpétué"

Introduced in 1965, "Pink Perpétué" is a cross between "Danse du Feu" and "New Dawn". It is not a rampant grower, taking several years to reach much above 8ft (2.4m), and it is ideally suited to a pillar, which it will clothe from top to bottom in flowers and foliage. The foliage has good disease resistance, is fairly glossy, quite large and on the dark side of mid-green. It comes into flower a little later than average, but the first flowering is very profuse. The medium sized flowers have over twenty petals and they are a pleasantly rounded form, with each flower well displayed in the truss. The mid-pink petals with carmine on the reverse are stable and have no unpleasant fade. The overall colour effect can be rather harsh. After the first flush several intermittent blooms will be produced before a really outstanding crop in the autumn. This is often as good as the first flush, particularly if the rose has been thoroughly dead-headed after the first flowering. There is a tangy, but not strong, fruity fragrance.

"Rosarium Uetersen"

Introduced as recently as 1977, "Rosarium Uetersen" is establishing itself in Europe but is not yet well known in the United Kingdom or the U.S.A. It is another of the climbing roses descended from *R. kordesii* and was bred from "Karlsruhe" crossed with a seedling. "Karlsruhe", which is directly descended from *R. kordesii*, is a many-petalled pink climber and has passed on many of its best qualities to "Rosarium Uetersen".

"Rosarium Uetersen" is a very adaptable rose and may be successfully grown on wall or pillar; it is also sufficiently pliant to make a large and impressive weeping standard. It will comfortably attain 10ft (3m) on a wall. The delightfully shiny, light to medium green foliage is very profuse. The leaves have deeply toothed incisions and are very large. There is a wealth of bloom at the first flowering, which is usually around mid-summer. The fairly large flowers, which are mid-pink tending towards salmon with comparatively little colour fade, are packed with up to 140 petals. The flowers are rounded but when fully open are flat with a very pretty irregularity to the petals. The indications to date are that this rose will repeat very satisfactorily. The fragrance, which has been likened to sweet green apples, is notable.

"Rosy Mantle"

Introduced in 1968, "Rosy Mantle" won a trial ground certificate from England's Royal National Rose Society in 1970. Its parents were "New Dawn" pollinated by "Prima Ballerina", a large-flowered pink with good freedom of flower and a lovely perfume, and from it "Rosy Mantle" inherited colour, scent and fine flower form.

"Rosy Mantle" can be grown in most situations, and it is equally successful on wall or pergola although it does need careful management or it will become rather bare at the base. It will reach 10ft (3m) on a wall and about 8ft (2.4m) against a pillar. The dark green, glossy foliage has a good health record, but it is not outstandingly profuse. The first flowers make a very good display. The blooms are quite large and of good form, with the outer petals opening wide while the bud form is maintained at the centre of the flower, an interesting and unusual petal formation. The petals are an attractive silver-pink, with the colour deepening towards the base. There is a good repeat flower display in autumn, and the sweet fragrance is pleasant if not outstanding. If you have an older plant, you will have to cut back one stem close to the base to help overcome the plant's tendency to produce stems with no leaves for several feet.

"Royal Gold"

For magnificence of the individual bloom, this climber must be very close to the best. But one fine bloom does not necessarily mean that the rose is worth growing, and there are problems associated with "Royal Gold". Raised and introduced in the United States in 1957, it is a cross between climbing "Goldilocks" and "Lydia"; climbing "Goldilocks" has contributed the climbing habit and repeat flower and "Lydia", a bright golden-yellow large flowered but not very reliable rose, has contributed the colour and unreliability.

"Royal Gold" must be grown in a warm, protected site, ideally against a south wall although a well sheltered pillar may succeed. In a suitable environment, 10ft (3m) of growth is attainable, but it may not grow much over 5ft (1.5m) for several years. The dark, semi-glossy foliage gives the plant a good covering. In spring there will not be a big display, clusters of two or three blooms on a stem being scattered over the plant. The full-petalled blooms are quite large, 4in (10cm) across, and they are a stunning rich, deep golden-yellow. There is a tangy fragrance, unusual and appealing. Sporadic clusters of blooms are produced for much of the season, but there will never be a large spread.

"Royal Sunset"

This fine, American-raised climber, which achieved the high rating of 8.1 in a fairly recent U.S. poll, is virtually unknown in the United Kingdom. The parents were the climber "Sungold" and the popular and fragrant "Sutters Gold". "Sungold" itself was bred from two climbers – "Margaret Anderson" and climbing "Souvenir de Claudius Pernet".

"Royal Sunset" has dark, leathery foliage, a considerable improvement on "Sutters Gold". Predominantly upright in habit, growth of 8ft (2.4m) on a pillar or 10ft (3m) on a wall may be expected. The flowers are quite large, up to 5in (13cm) across, and have about twenty petals. The cup-shaped flowers open an attractive shade of apricot, but the colour is not stable and the blooms turn pink. There is a pleasant, fruity fragrance. The rose is reported to flower freely and to produce good repeat blooms.

"Schoolgirl"

Like "Royal Gold", a single bloom of "Schoolgirl" flatters to deceive. Shapely, with attractive and unusual colouring and quite a nice scent, the plant has some faults as well.

Bred by Sam McGredy, it is a cross between "Coral Dawn" and "Belle Blonde". "Coral Dawn" is a descendant of "New Dawn", although its coral pink flowers are slightly larger than those of "New Dawn" and it does not climb as well. "Belle Blonde" is a world-renowned large-flowered yellow rose raised by Francis Meilland.

After its introduction in 1964, "Schoolgirl" slowly gained popularity, eventually reaching sixth position in the tables issued by England's Royal National Rose Society (R.N.R.S.). In the last few years, however, it has lost some of its admirers, and it has never been especially popular in the United States.

"Schoolgirl" is not a temperamental grower, and it will climb in most situations, reaching 10ft (3m) on a wall. The large, dark green and glossy foliage may need spraying to keep blackspot at bay. The flowers are beautifully shaped at the bud stage, and as they expand, the flowers reveal an exciting apricot-orange shade on a bloom that is the size of many large flowered bush roses. There is a good spread of bloom at the first flowering, although it cannot in any sense be called a profuse flowerer, and while "Schoolgirl" goes on producing blooms at intervals, one is left with the wish that it would produce more. There is some scent, but it is not particularly attractive. In full sun the blooms fade quickly, until they look a washed-out salmon-pink. And to add to its faults, older plants become very bare and unattractive at the base.

"Sensass Delbard" and "Messire Delbard"

These two roses are very similar, but both are virtually unknown in the United Kingdom and in the United States, which I feel is a pity.

"Sensass Delbard" does not climb as well as "Messire", and it will take a few years to exceed 8ft (2.4m). It has very healthy, mid-green foliage, flowers freely and produces good repeat blooms. The bright red flowers do not have a great deal of scent.

"Messire Delbard", on the other hand, will reach a height of 10ft (3m) on a wall. The plentiful, leathery and shiny dark green foliage is very resistant to disease. Early into flower, with quite large trusses on each stem, the plant becomes very well covered with bloom. Tight buds open to globular flowers, which are predominantly carmine-red but have deeper, more velvety edges to the petals. The flowers, up to 4in (10cm) across, have nearly forty petals, which cause the stems to nod under their weight. Perfume is virtually non-existent, but the flowers last a long time and remain attractive. There is a good second flush in the early autumn with some flowers between.

"Summer Wine" *or* "Korizont"

Winning a trial ground certificate as recently as 1983, this new rose is already being stocked by several U.K. nurserymen, and it seems certain that more will follow as it becomes better known. The seed parent was "Coral Dawn", but the pollen parent was a seedling derived from "Zitronenfalter" pollinated by "Clare Grammerstorf". "Zitronenfalter" is a healthy yellow shrub rose, and "Clare Grammerstorf" is a light yellow shrub with distinctive light green foliage, which has produced a number of successful roses.

"Summer Wine" is a vigorous climber and will probably exceed 10ft (3m) in height. The foliage is light green in the early stages, but it darkens somewhat, eventually turning semi-glossy. Although the medium sized, faintly scented flowers have only a double row of petals, the open flowers are truly beautiful: soft coral pink blooms are enhanced by a yellow centre, which displays red anthers and filaments. The repeat flowers are satisfactory, but it seems unlikely that there will be a profusion of blooms at any one time.

"Swan Lake"

There are very few repeat-flowering white climbing roses, and "Swan Lake", which is stocked by many U.K. nurserymen, is undoubtedly the most popular white climber available here. A cross between "Memoriam" and "Heidelberg", it was introduced by Sam McGredy in 1968. "Memoriam" is a beautiful large flowered white rose with a pink centre, and although it is a little temperamental as a grower, its colouring and beauty of form have been almost exactly matched by "Swan Lake".

Predominantly upright in character, "Swan Lake" grows slowly, although it should achieve a height of 10ft (3m) on a wall. It is perhaps best grown, however, as a 7–8ft (2.4m) pillar rose. The glossy, dark green foliage is plentiful, and

looks good until mildew and blackspot strike. If you are considering growing this rose, you will certainly need to spray against blackspot and probably against mildew also.

In a normal year, "Swan Lake" will be in flower early; its first crop is generally very good with both individual blooms and quite large clusters. The creamy buds open to very full, beautifully formed flowers, which, when expanded, are white with a soft pink centre. Most white roses struggle in the wet, but this one excels and suffers little or no petal damage. After the first flowering, trusses of bloom are produced at intervals so that the plant is rarely without flower. There is a light but not very significant fragrance.

"Sympathie"

Introduced in 1964 from the Kordes nursery, "Sympathie" is classified as a Kordesii although it is in fact one generation removed from *R. kordesii*. The parentage is "Wilhelm Hansman" pollinated by "Don Juan". "Wilhelm Hansman" arose from a seedling, "Baby Château", crossed with "Else Poulsen", which in its turn was pollinated by *R. kordesii*. "Wilhelm Hansman" is dark red and free flowering and it has passed on many of its characteristics to "Sympathie".

A perpetual climber, "Sympathie" must be one of the strongest if not *the* strongest grower. It should comfortably reach 15ft (4.6m) on a wall, where it grows as much laterally as it does upwards. The thick, dark green foliage is glossy but unfortunately, it is prone to blackspot. The first flowering is profuse, most stems producing medium sized clusters. The blooms are up to 4in (10cm) across with over twenty petals, and at its best the colouring is a superb dark, velvety red; however, it can be rather variable, and, like most roses, it needs sunshine to give of its best. After the first flush there is usually something of a gap, but certainly by early autumn another large crop of flowers is produced. Although there is quite a strong fragrance, it is a typical Kordesii and therefore rather a bitter-sweet affair. Older plants become rather leggy, and careful training and pruning are essential.

"Westerland"

Introduced in 1969 by Kordes from a cross between "Friedrich Wörlein" and "Circus", "Westerland" is often classified as a shrub, and with pruning can be grown in this way, but it has greater willingness to leap upwards than many classified as climbers.

The vigorous growth shown by "Westerland" must be largely attributed to "Clare Grammerstorf", one of the parents of "Friedrich Wörlein". Against a pillar "Westerland" will attain 8ft (2.4m) and with a wall as support, growth over 10ft (3m) may be expected. The foliage is large, bronzy when new, eventually turning a deep glossy green. It is slightly prone to mildew but shows excellent resistance to blackspot. The first flowers appear relatively early in the season, and there is a large display, with 4in (10cm) blooms produced in medium sized clusters.

Colour varies considerably with the season, ranging between orange, orange-red and yellow. Even though the old flowers turn pink, they remain attractive at all stages. A large second flush can be expected, with many blooms produced from the base of the plant and large trusses borne on the basal shoots. There is a strong and satisfying sweet, fruity fragrance.

"White Cockade"

The offspring of the mainly pink "New Dawn" and of the yellow and orange "Circus" turned out to be white, but it is a very fine semi-climber. Introduced by Alec Cocker in 1969, "White Cockade" is popular in the United States as well as in the United Kingdom. Best grown against a low fence or pillar, its restrained growth is ideal for a smaller garden, and it rarely achieves more than 7ft (2.1m) in height.

The glossy foliage is proving to have above average disease resistance. The first flowers appear in mid-season, and they are profuse and borne evenly throughout the plant. The semi-double flowers have a good form with a pretty stamen display when they are fully expanded. Overall the rose appears to be almost pure white, but closer inspection reveals hints of pink and cream. The autumn flowering is very satisfactory, and there is a pleasant, if not remarkable, fragrance.

RECOMMENDED VARIETIES

Most vigorous

Albéric Barbier
Very profuse flowering; shiny foliage; some later blooms

R.b. banksiae
Not free flowering in the U.K.; magnificent in warm countries; sweet scent

R.b. lutea
Free flowering; early in flower; lovely foliage

R. brunonii La Mortola
Grey-green foliage; slightly tender; exceptional vigour

R. filipes Kiftsgate
Masses of flower; exceptional vigour

R. gigantea
Very large single flowers; best in warm districts

R. helenae
Beautiful flowering trusses; masses of hips

Mermaid
Large, very beautiful single flowers; wicked thorns; brittle stems

R. mulliganii
Lovely foliage; very vigorous; masses of flower

Paul's Himalayan Musk
Very vigorous; pliant stems, excellent for growing into trees

R. rubus
Sweet scent; good hip display

R. sinowilsonii
Magnificent foliage; needs a warm site

Medium height

Compassion
Fragrant; free flowering; good repeat

Danse du Feu
Very free flowering; fades badly

Desprez à Fleur Jaune
Old-fashioned look; very free flowering; fragrant

Handel
Very distinctive flowers; good repeat

Iskra (Sparkling Scarlet)
Attractive bright colouring

John Cabot
Healthy; free flowering; novel colour

Mme. Alfred Carrière
Very profuse first flowering; fragrant; some repeat

New Dawn
Healthy; free flowering; fragrant

Parade
Rather a harsh pink; very good repeat

Parkdirektor Riggers
Bright colour; excellent repeat

Rosarium Uetersen
Very full flowers; profuse flowering

Sympathie
Bright colour; good repeat; may become leggy

Short growers

Aloha
Very healthy; ugly buds turn into lovely flowers

Dublin Bay
Free flowering; good colour; good repeat

Galway Bay
Erect grower; free flowering; spray for black spot

Golden Showers
Slightly loose, but very free, flowers; excellent repeat

Joseph's Coat
Shrub or climber; very colourful

Morgengrüss
Healthy; fragrant; tough

Nozomi
Masses of dainty flowers; very little repeat

Pink Perpétué
Rather harsh pink; excellent repeat

Royal Gold
Superb colour; needs a warm spot

Sensass Delbard
Very good colour; healthy; free flowering

Westerland
Fragrant; lovely colour; deserves more recognition

White Cockade
Very healthy; good repeat; deserves more recognition

North walls

Albéric Barbier
Hardy; vigorous
Dortmund
Hardy; free flowering; good repeat
François Juranville
Good scent; vigorous
Leverkusen
Hardy; free flowering; slow to repeat
Mme. Alfred Carrière
Very profuse first flowering; some later bloom
Mme. Grégoire Staechelin
Magnificent outpouring of bloom; only one crop
Maigold
Excellent first flowering; a few later blooms
New Dawn
Scented; good repeat; hardy
Parkdirektor Riggers
Very good repeat bloom; hardy
Rosy Mantle
Nice colour; good repeat; guard against legginess
Sympathie
Bright colour; quite hardy; good repeat
Veilchenblau
Colouring at its best in a shady position

Early flowerers
(Special characteristics in the United Kingdom)

Alister Stella Gray
Needs a warm site; in flower before mid-summer
Allen Chandler
Nice colour; some repeat; early summer flowering
R.b. banksiae
In flower in May (earlier in hot countries)
R.b. lutea
Best choice for early flowers in south of U.K.
Climbing Crimson Glory
First flowers in May
Climbing Mme. Edouard Herriot
Late May in south; before mid-summer in most districts
Desprez à Fleur Jaune
Before mid-summer
Emily Gray
May–June
Gloire de Dijon
May in south of U.K.
Golden Showers
Usually before mid-June
Lawrence Johnston
Beginning of June
Maigold
Mid-May onwards

Fragrance

Albertine
Sweet fruity scent
R.b. banksiae
Sweet violet scent
Climbing Crimson Glory
Rich damask
Climbing Ena Harkness
Variable, but at its best very powerful
Compassion
Strong and heady; occasionally floats in the air
Mme. Grégoire Staechelin
Very sweet scent, always attractive
Maigold
Spicy, soapy fragrance, very enticing
New Dawn
Fruity like apples
R. rubus
Cast freely into the air, usually after mid-day
Veilchenblau
Sweet violets, cast freely into the air
Westerland
Strong fruity scent
Zéphirine Drouhin
Sweet damask-like scent

Late flowerers
(Special characteristics
in the United Kingdom)
American Pillar
End of June
R. bracteata
July–August
Climbing Cécile Brunner
End of June
Crimson Shower
July
Félicité et Perpétué
July
R. filipes Kiftsgate
Mid-July
R. gentiliana
Early July
R. helenae
Early July
R. mulliganii
July
Purity
July
R. wichuraiana
July–August
Veilchenblau
Early July

Hips
Bantry Bay
Nearly all flowers set seed;
remove them if you want
more flowers
Dortmund
Bright red hips; remove them
if you want more flowers
R. filipes Kiftsgate
Large bunches of round hips
turning colour September
R. helenae
The star of the hip world
R. kordesii
Large hips
Mme. Grégoire Staechelin
Nearly every flower sets seed;
large hips
Maigold
A few later flowers or hips –
take your choice
Meg
Huge hips
Morgengrüss
Attractively elongated hips
R. mulliganii
Masses of tiny hips
Parkdirektor Riggers
Masses of hips, turning colour
late autumn
R. rubus
Lovely waxy, small, dark red
hips

GARDENS TO VISIT

Interesting collections of climbing roses may be seen at the following gardens:

United Kingdom

Bowood House,
   Calne, Wiltshire
Castle Howard,
   York
Cliveden,
   near Maidenhead,
   Berkshire
Dixon Park,
   Belfast, Northern Ireland
Haddon Hall,
   Bakewell, Derbyshire
Hidcote Manor,
   Chipping Campden,
   Gloucestershire
Hyde Hall,
   Chelmsford, Essex
Kew Gardens,
   Richmond, Surrey
Kiftsgate Court,
   Chipping Campden,
   Gloucestershire
Lime Kiln Rosarium,
   near Ipswich, Suffolk
Mottisfont,
   near Romsey, Hampshire
Mount Stewart,
   Newtownards, Co. Down,
   Northern Ireland
Nymans,
   near Crawley, Sussex
Polesden Lacey,
   near Dorking, Surrey
Rosemoor,
   Great Torrington, Devon
Rowallane Garden,
   Saintfield, Co. Down,
   Northern Ireland
St Albans,
   Headquarters of the R.N.R.S.,
   Hertfordshire

Savill Gardens,
   Windsor, Berkshire
Sissinghurst,
   near Cranbrook, Kent
Tintinhull,
   near Yeovil, Somerset
Wallington Hall,
   Morpeth, Northumberland
Wisley,
   Headquarters of the Royal
   Horticultural
   Society, Woking, Surrey

United States

American Rose Center,
   Shreveport, Louisiana
Berkley Rose Garden,
   California
Boerner Botanical Gardens,
   Hales Corner, Wisconsin
Brooklyn Botanic Garden,
   Brooklyn, New York
Columbus Park of Roses,
   Columbus, Ohio
Descanso Gardens,
   La Canada, California
Edisto Gardens, Orangeburg,
   South Carolina
Elizabeth Park Rose Garden,
   Hartford, Connecticut
E de T Bechtel Memorial Rose
   Garden, Botanical Gardens,
   New York
Exposition Park Rose Garden,
   Los Angeles, California
Hershey Rose Gardens and
   Arboretum, Pennsylvania
Huntington Rose Garden,
   San Marino, California
Idlewild Park, Reno, Nevada

International Rose Test
   Garden, Portland, Oregon
Lakeside Rose Garden,
   Fort Wayne, Indiana
Longwood Gardens,
   Kennett Square,
   Pennsylvania
Manito Gardens,
   Spokane, Washington
Maplewood Park Rose
   Garden, Rochester, New
   York
Missouri Botanic Gardens,
   St Louis, Missouri
Municipal Rose Garden,
   Kansas City, Missouri
Municipal Rose Garden,
   Oakland, California
Municipal Rose Garden,
   San José, California
Municipal Rose Garden,
   Tulsa, Oklahoma
Municipal Rose Garden,
   Tyler, Texas
Pageant of Roses Garden,
   Whittier, California
Queens Botanic Garden,
   Flushing, New York
Ritter Park Garden,
   Huntington, West Virginia
Rose and Test Garden,
   Topeka, Kansas
Roses of Legend & Romance
   Garden, Wooster, Ohio
Samuell-Grand Rose Garden,
   Dallas, Texas
Tennessee Botanical Gardens,
   Cheekwood, Nashville,
   Tennessee

GLOSSARY

Budding the means by which nearly all roses are propagated. In this process the growth bud of a garden rose is inserted into the rootstock of a wild or species rose to create a more vigorous bush that will produce more growth and more flowers. Many nurserymen use as their budding stock *R. laxa (R. coriifolia froebelii)*, which has a straight neck, few thorns and produces few suckers, but up to a dozen different stocks are used in different parts of the United Kingdom.

Budding involves removing with a sharp knife a bud, which is found between the leaf and the stem, and inserting it into the neck of the rootstock. Make a sloping, T-shaped cut in the neck of the rootstock, fold back the bark and push the bud into the space. Ensure that the join is airtight by fastening a rubber tie over the cut.

In the last few years a new technique, called micro-propagation or tissue culture, by which large numbers of any variety can be produced very quickly, has been tried with roses. As these roses are dependent on their own root systems, it seems unlikely that they will enjoy a great success in the garden.

Climbing rose a name used to describe a multitude of roses of various classifications with climbing characteristics or which can be used as climbers.

Hybrid a cross-pollination between two different roses. For example, if "Handel" were pollinated by "Dublin Bay", the resulting seedlings would be hybrids. Similarly, seedlings resulting if *R. multiflora* (a species) were pollinated by *R. helenae* (also a species) would be hybrids because, although they would be similar, none of them would be identical.

Miniature climbers roses that have narrower stems, smaller foliage and flowers less than 2in (5cm) across. This is a fairly recent development, although with obvious potential for today's smaller gardens. Among many of note to appear so far have been the hybrids developed by Ralph Moore – climbing "Jackie", "Pink Cameo" and "Red Cascade" – but Ernest Williams from Texas has produced some interesting possibilities, while "Nozomi" from Toru Onodera is a delight.

Ramblers roses that, if left alone, will spread freely in all directions, hooking their way into, and climbing through, nearby hedges or trees. Most ramblers have only a short burst of profuse flowering, and most have been replaced by more recently produced climbers, which flower at intervals during the growing season. Ramblers have lax, pliant stems, which rise from the base of the plant each year and can make 15ft (4.6m) of growth each season. In one respect they resemble raspberry canes, which produce their flowers and fruit on the wood that grew the previous year. To get maximum vigour into the new season's growth, raspberry canes should be cut back to the base as soon as they have finished fruiting. Most true rambling roses need to be treated in the same way. However, many nurserymen tend to group together all summer-flowering roses and call them ramblers. A large number of these and those with stiffer stems do not need pruning after flowering. Always find out the specific requirements of each variety that you grow.

Repeat- and perpetual-flowering climbers A small proportion of the seedlings resulting from the cross-pollination of once-flowering climbers with repeat-flowering bushes were repeat-flowering climbers. Such roses usually had a large crop of flowers at the first, summer flowering, then a gap until the autumn, when a second, smaller crop was produced. So much cross-breeding has taken place in the last 150 years that one or two climbing roses have reached the stage of being almost constantly or perpetually in flower. Rose nurserymen tend to group all repeat-flowering climbing roses together and call them perpetual; in fact they are not always in flower, and the only two climbers most nearly approaching perpetual flowering are "Golden Showers" and "Parade".

Scrambling climbers roses that "scramble" into anything their thorns can reach – shrubs, hedges, small and large trees. It is nearly always a mistake to plant them in a small garden unless there is considerable space next door and your neighbour is likely to welcome your generosity. Typical examples are *R. mulliganii*, *R. rubus*, *R. helenae*, *R. filipes* and *R. gigantea*.

Short climbers more recent introductions that are ideally suited for smaller gardens. If space is limited and there is only a 6ft (1.8m) fence or wall, a climbing rose that can be easily kept within its allotted space is ideal. The most popular short climber is "Golden Showers", but "Aloha", "Dublin Bay" and "Pink Perpétué" are equally suitable.

Species a rose (or other plant variety) that will reproduce itself identically from its own seed. For instance, when planted, seed of *R. multiflora* will produce *R. multiflora*.

Sport or mutation a flowering shoot of a different colour from the rest of the plant. The shoot supporting this flower can be propagated and a new variety of rose may thus occur. More often than not sports are of inferior quality and do not go into commercial production, but a recent successful sport is "L'Oreal Trophy", which originated on "Alexander". Here the vermilion colouring of "Alexander" changed to the orange of "L'Oreal Trophy". Sports can also appear because nearly all bush roses have climbing ancestors, and very occasionally a long shoot will arise from a bush rose. If this shoot is propagated successfully, a climbing sport with a possible commercial future will have been produced. Generally, these climbing sports are not very free flowering and there are few or no repeat flowers.

Summer- or once-flowering climber All the first climbing roses were once flowering, and when hybridists first started to interfere, the first hybrids were all once flowering. This flowering period will vary with each variety, some lasting for only three weeks while others will be in flower for nearly two months. Almost all flowering plants can easily reproduce themselves, but until quite recently all roses flowered only once. It was natural that this should be so because the rose flowered, set seed and then put all its energy into maturing the seed. A few hundred years ago, but nobody is sure when, a rose that flowered more than once was discovered growing in China. It would have been prized and protected and no doubt distributed to interested gardeners. This China rose was responsible, after many generations, for all of today's roses. But of course repeat flowering is defeating nature; no longer is the energy of the plant solely concentrated on ripening seed.

Synstylae a family of roses in which the style (the stalk linking the ovary and stigma of a female flower) is a single, fused column and not, as is more usual, a series of columns.

Variety or cultivar An individual rose is traditionally known as a variety. Recently some authorities have replaced the word "variety" with "cultivar", which is held to be a more accurate description.

SOCIETIES

If you already love roses or if you find your interest in roses is increasing, join one of the specialist rose societies, which flourish in almost every European country as well as in the United States, Australia, Canada, New Zealand, Japan, South Africa and India.

The Royal National Rose Society has its headquarters at Chiswell Green Lane, St Albans, Hertfordshire. Here is to be seen one of the very finest displays of roses in the world. Even if you do not become a member, you certainly ought to visit the gardens.

The American Rose Society can be joined by application to: PO Box 30000, Shreveport, Louisiana 71130.

If you become fascinated by hybridizing, you should think about joining one of the specialist amateur groups that exist in America, New Zealand and the United Kingdom. The Rose Hybridizers Association, which has a membership from all over the world, can be contacted through its Secretary Larry D. Peterson, 3245 Wheaton Road, Horseheads, New York 14845. The New Zealand Rose Breeders Association also has members from around the world. It can be contacted through Mrs Christine Ford, 280 Tremain Avenue, Palmerston North, New Zealand. The Amateur Rose Breeders Association has overseas as well as British members. It can be contacted through the Secretary Mr D. Everitt, 48 Shrewsbury Fields, Shifnal, Shropshire.

BIBLIOGRAPHY

U.K. publications

Those titles marked * are particularly useful on climbing roses

Allen, R. C., **Roses for Every Garden**, M. Barrows, New York

Bean, W. J., **Trees and Shrubs Hardy in the British Isles** (8th edition), John Murray, London

Buckley, F., **Germination of Rose Achenes**, Amateur Rose Breeders Association

Bunyard, E. A., **Old Garden Roses**, Collingridge

Cox, E. H. M., **Plant Hunting in China**, William Collins, London and Glasgow

Edwards, G., **Wild and Old Garden Roses**,* David & Charles, Newton Abbot

Farrer, R., **On the Eaves of the World**, Edward Arnold, London

Foster-Melliar, Rev. A. and Molyneux, Herbert, **The Book of the Rose** (4th edition),* Macmillan, London

Gault, S. M. and Synge, P. M., **The Dictionary of Roses in Colour**,* Michael Joseph, London

Gibson, M., **Shrub Roses, Climbers and Ramblers**, William Collins, London and Glasgow

Harkness, J., **Roses**, Dent, London

Harkness, J., **The Makers of Heavenly Roses**, Souvenir Press, London

Harvey, N. P., **The Rose in Britain**, Souvenir Press, London

Hole, S. R. Dean, **A Book about Roses**,* Blackwood, London

Hollis, L., **Roses**, Collingridge, London

Jekyll, G. and Mawley, E., **Roses for English Gardens***

Kordes, W., **Roses**,* Studio Vista, London

Krussman, G., **Roses**, * Batsford, London

Le Grice, E., **Rose Growing Complete**,* Faber & Faber, London

Macself, A. J., **The Rose Grower's Treasury**, Collingridge

Moore, R. S., **All about Miniature Roses**, Diversity Books, Kansas

McGredy, S. and Jennett, S., **A Family of Roses**

Park, B., **Collins Guide to Roses**, William Collins, London and Glasgow

Paul, W., **The Rose Garden**, Simpkin, Hamilton, Marshall

Poulsen, S., **Poulsen on the Rose**, MacGibbon Kee, London

Royal National Rose Society, **Annuals** from 1913 to the present

Shepherd, R., **History of the Rose**,* Macmillan, New York

Thomas, G. S., **Climbing Roses Old and New**,* Phoenix House

Thomas, G. S., **The Old Shrub Roses**, Phoenix House

Thomas, G. S., **Shrub Roses of Today**, Phoenix House

Wheatcroft, H., **In Praise of Roses**, Barrie & Jenkins

Wilson, H. van Pelt, **Climbing Roses***

Young, N. **The Complete Rosarian**, Hodder & Stoughton, London

U.S. publications

Bunyard, Edward A., **Old Garden Roses**, Earl M. Coleman Enterprises, Inc., Crugers, New York, 1978.

Edwards, Gordon, **Wild and Old Garden Roses**, Sweetbrier Press, Palo Alto, California, 1975.

Fitch, Charles M., **The Complete Book of Miniature Roses**, E. P. Dutton, New York, 1980.

Gibson, Michael, **Growing Roses**, Timber Press, Portland, Oregon, 1984.

Jekyll, Gertrude, and Mawley, Edward, **Roses** (originally titled **Roses for English Gardens**), Ayer Co. Publications, Inc., Salem, New Hampshire, 1982.

Krussman, Gerd, **The Complete Book of Roses** (originally titled **Roses**), Timber Press, Portland, Oregon, 1981.

Paul, William, **The Rose Garden**, Earl M. Coleman Enterprises, Inc., Crugers, New York, 1978.

Shepherd, Roy E., **History of the Rose**, Earl M. Coleman Enterprises, Inc., Crugers, New York, 1978.

INDEX

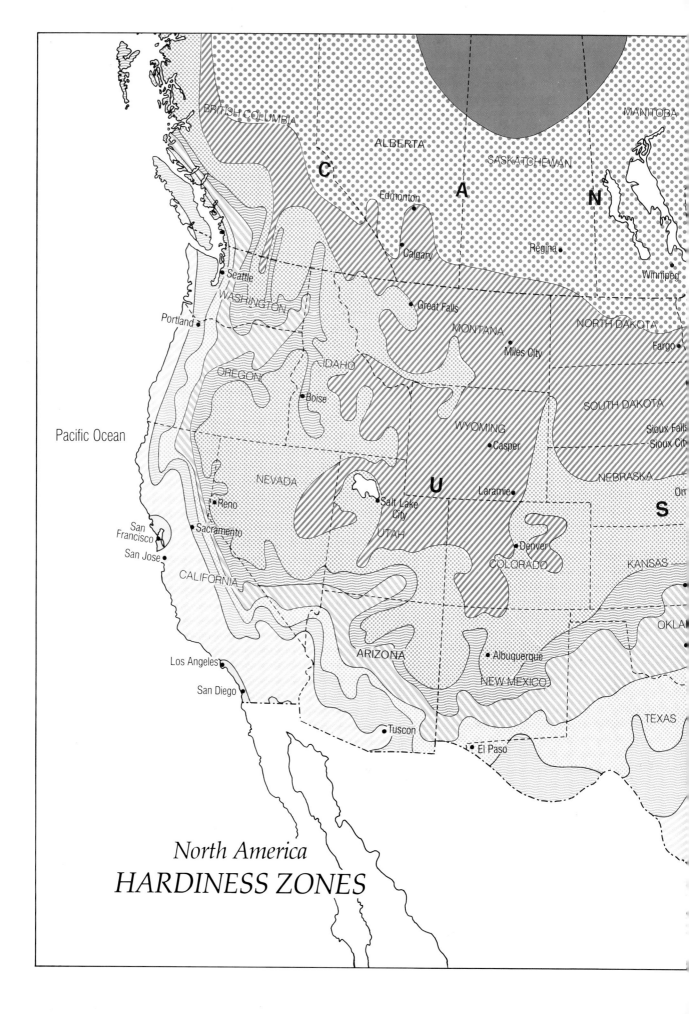

North America
HARDINESS ZONES